Divine INTERVENTION

HOPE AND HELP FOR FAMILIES OF ADDICTS

Mark E. Shaw

Divine
INTERVENTION

HO
FAN

Copyright 2007

Scripture references are quoted from
The English Standard Version of the Bible
and where noted,
The King James Version
and The New King James Version

Cover design by Melanie Schmidt

ISBN 1-885904-63-0

PRINTED IN THE UNITED STATES OF AMERICA
BY
FOCUS PUBLISHING
Bemidji, Minnesota

PREFACE

As someone who has been personally touched by addiction, it is my passionate desire to see individuals overcome self-destructive, addictive thinking and behaving. Having witnessed families, marriages, friendships, and other intimate relationships being devastated by addictive behavior, I possess an even more intense desire to help those who are not addicted themselves, but who have loved ones that are ensnared in the trap of addiction. It is for this group that this book was written.

The main purpose of this book is to bring encouragement and hope to you: the friend, family member, spouse, and loved one of the addict. Another purpose is to teach you biblical principles to challenge your thinking about addiction, and enable you to best help your addicted loved one in a biblical manner.

Because of your love, you may find it difficult to help your addicted loved one. You cannot trust your feelings, but you can trust the Word of God and the leading of the Holy Spirit. God is sovereign and there is nothing He cannot do. If something is His will, it will happen. I recommend that you not trust in yourself, but trust in the Lord your God who is omnipotent (all-powerful). I encourage you to follow His principles from His Word that are illuminated and taught to you by the Holy Spirit that lives within you.

Obviously, I cannot counsel you through every step of the process of helping your addicted loved one. However, God can and will, but you have to 'get out of the way' while remembering that He alone is God. You cannot be god to your loved one, but you can be an instrument that the Lord will use if He so chooses.

As you read this book, understand that these principles are intended to teach, rebuke, correct, and train you to think and act rightly in your relationship with God and in your relationship with your addicted loved one.[1] You will be required to apply some of these biblical principles; it will not be easy. However, the more you seek to glorify God and do things His way, the more you will grow into the likeness and image of Christ, while giving your loved one the best opportunity to overcome the addiction.

Seek biblical counsel from your pastor, church leaders, or trusted

---

[1] 2 Timothy 3:16-17.

Divine Intervention

Christian friend. Allow the Holy Spirit to make you both willing and able to seek His will and apply these biblical principles in your life. Each person's situation is different, so it is impossible for me to address all possible scenarios, but I have confidence in God's Word and the Holy Spirit's guidance to accomplish His sovereign plan and purpose in your situation.

Pray, read your Bible, seek godly counsel, face your heart issues, and practice these challenging principles in your relationship with the addicted loved one, and you will see God's grace, love, truth, goodness, sovereignty, justice, and peace. You will learn so much about the Lord and how He loves you through this trial in your life, but you must do so His way or you may miss the blessings of God. The Lord requires you to obey Him in all things because He knows it is best for you and it gives Him glory. Do so today!

Mark E. Shaw

DEDICATION

This book is dedicated to Mary, my wife and best friend;
Ronny and Sandra, my parents and wonderful friends
now that I am grown; and Don Bowen, my beloved
friend and NANC counselor.

TABLE OF CONTENTS

Divine Intervention

INTRODUCTION: WHAT DO I DO?

In the heart of an addict, there is a self-centered, sinful, and willful desire to fulfill an appetite that causes them to neglect God-given responsibilities and/or to commit harmful acts toward others and self. Rather than an actual physical heart, the word "heart," in the Bible means the inner essence of mankind containing all desires, attitudes, emotions, and *thinking*.[2] The addict's thinking is the initial key that triggers addictive behavior and must be changed for them to have success in battling the addiction. An "addiction" is a physical symptom of a deeper, spiritual problem of the heart called "idolatry" in the Bible.[3]

An addict's body has become physically dependent on the desired pleasure through the repeated process of experiencing it. Addictions come in many idolatrous pleasures including drugs, alcohol, sex, homosexual acts, food, gambling, sleep, television watching, internet usage, video game playing, exercise, shopping, spending money, self-injury, and "cutting" oneself. And there are more! All of these outward manifestations of idolatry can become "physically addictive" in that one's body adapts and adjusts to the physical fulfillment of the appetite and requires more in order to experience the original amount of pleasure. It's the same, never satiated, empty, temporary pleasure that is always promised by sin. One pastor has eloquently likened sinful desires to that wonderful confection found at any state or county fair – cotton candy. Sugar coated air! It looks and smells so inviting as you walk near it, but once you put it in your mouth, poof! Nothing! No substance! It's gone![4]

Some people have difficulty understanding how shopping and video game playing are addictive because they have never struggled with that particular addiction. But that's the key. Any pleasure, even good pleasures like sexual intimacy in marriage, can become addictive behavior in the thinking and acting of a person whose body begins to physiologically desire and demand that the pleasure be fulfilled repeatedly to the harm of others and self. In this way, any outward

---

[2] Here are just a few references to the "heart" from the book of Luke alone: 5:22, 6:45, 8:12, 9:47, 10:27, 12:34, 21:34, 24:32, 24:38.

[3] Shaw, Mark, The Heart of Addiction, Milestone Books Publishing, Vestavia Hills, AL, p vii.

[4] Obtained from sermon taught by Pastor/Teacher Harry Reeder on February 11, 2007, at Briarwood Presbyterian Church.

behavior can be addictive mentally and often physiologically.[5]

Here's an excerpt from <u>The Heart of Addiction</u> that best defines addiction:

> "Quite simply, physical addiction occurs when you satisfy a natural appetite and desire with a temporary pleasure repeatedly until you become the servant of the temporary object of pleasure rather than its master. Addiction is likened to slavery and idolatry in the Bible. You use the temporarily pleasurable substance to escape, but in reality you find that you are enslaved rather than free. Human beings love an "escape" because it seems so freeing, but addiction is a trap that lets you think that you will be "free" when you really become a "slave." God created you to have liberty in Christ, but that freedom from the slavery of sin was not without cost. It cost the Son of God His life on the cross.
>
> If you eliminate the word "compulsive" from the worldly definition for "addiction" and replace it with "habitual," then you can better use this word, "addiction." When you make this change, addiction is redefined as the "persistent *habitual* use of a substance known by the user to be harmful." Once this new definition is in place, addiction becomes a word more closely resembling the life-devastating sin of drunkenness described in the Bible. When the word "addiction" is used in the remainder of this book, it will refer to this redefined and new definition since it is biblically more accurate. The new definition of addiction also brings more hope to the suffering Christian addict. Because ungodly, destructive habits can be replaced by godly, productive habits, there is hope. Real and lasting change can and will occur in your life."[6]

---

[5] For more about the heart attitudes and thoughts of the addicted mind, please refer to <u>The Heart of Addiction</u> by Mark E. Shaw.

[6] Shaw, Mark, <u>The Heart of Addiction</u>, Milestone Books Publishing, Vestavia Hills, AL, p 34-35.

As you walk through this study, you will learn to deal with the heart of the addict – the thinking, emotions, attitudes, and desires – so that a change occurs in the inner person. Otherwise, if the heart of the addict does not change, one outward, addictive behavior may cease while another addictive behavior replaces it, still leading to destruction. Only the Lord God has the power to change one's heart. Ezekiel 36:25-27 states: **"I will sprinkle clean water on you, and you shall be clean from all your uncleannesses, and from all your idols I will cleanse you. [26] And I will give you a new heart, and a new spirit I will put within you. And I will remove the heart of stone from your flesh and give you a heart of flesh. [27] And I will put my Spirit within you, and cause you to walk in my statutes and be careful to obey my rules."**

Your loved one who is addicted and caught in the trap of idolatry needs a new heart. Only God performs this type of heart surgery. God replaces the heart of stone with a heart of flesh and puts the Holy Spirit within the person. What a heart transplant that is! What a Surgeon the Lord is! Your addicted loved one needs radical surgery like this or the result will be self-destruction.

Common Scenarios

With this in mind, you may have asked some of the following questions:

- What do I do? My son is on crack cocaine.
- What do I do? My wife is strung out on pain pills and won't stop taking them.
- What do I do? My granddaughter goes out drinking every weekend and has two D.U.I. arrests already.
- What do I do? My husband disappears for three days at a time.
- What do I do? I pray but I can't seem to get my best friend to stop smoking pot.
- What do I do? My Christian friend thinks it is okay to abuse her prescription medication because it is prescribed by a doctor.
- What do I do? My son will play video games for hours at a time and lie about doing his homework. His grades are suffering as a result.
- What do I do? My daughter has hidden her homosexual lifestyle from me for the past few years until recently. She will not quit that lifestyle and is now drinking very heavily.

- What do I do? My brother-in-law is addicted to methamphetamines and is now committing all kinds of sexual sins. He is not the same person he used to be prior to this addiction.
- What do I do? My wife continues to spend money we do not have on excessive clothes and frivolous things for the children. She is out of control and we are headed for bankruptcy.
- What do I do? My boyfriend acts one way sometimes and like a totally different, evil person other times.

Family members and friends of an addicted loved one have asked these questions and countless others. As an addictions counselor, I get five times as many calls from those wanting to help an addicted loved one, (family members, employers, friends, and pastors) than I do from the addict. The addict rarely calls for help unless they are under some type of pressure due to the consequences of their behavior. That tells you that often the loved one is more concerned about the addict's self-destructive behavior than is the addict. The truth is that we must allow the addict to experience the pain of the terrible consequences of their sin.

Although different relationships require different approaches, you will see that many of the biblical principles explained here apply to the majority of relationships: spouses, parents, children, grandchildren, and friends. In this book, I have simplified the distinctions for you. In the first section, you will learn what you can do with an unwilling, unrepentant addicted loved one. In the second section, you will learn what you can do with a willing, repentant addicted loved one. In the third section of this book, you will learn some of the things the Lord desires to teach you the family member, friend, pastor, etc. through this trial, and how you can transform your hardships into blessings.

SECTION 1
UNWILLING AND UNREPENTANT ADDICTS

Divine Intervention

CHAPTER 1
THE MIND OF AN ADDICT

Do you ever wonder what is in the mind of an addict? Sometimes the addict himself wonders what is in his mind! Addiction puzzles most people because the very thoughts and behaviors of an addict are self-destructive. Why would someone want to destroy himself? Is he crazy? Does he have a so called "mental illness"?

Addiction of all types is becoming more prevalent in modern American culture. There is an emphasis in American culture upon pleasing self above all else. In the Bible, someone who seeks to please self more than to please the Lord is called an idolater. That word, "idolater," may seem like a foreign concept to you so let me explain idolatry a little further and it will become more clear.

What is Idolatry?

Idolatry is a sinful desire in the heart of an addict to please oneself. Idolatry takes a desire that can be either good or evil and turns it into a demand. Often, addicts want one (often both) of these two things: to experience pleasure or to escape pain. It is really that simple. The fulfillment of the addictive desire is only temporary; and because it is not lasting fulfillment, the addict desires to fulfill the appetite repeatedly. These unmet desires to experience pleasure overtake the addict; the demand for pleasure then dominates, and he or she thinks that this temporary fulfillment will bring happiness. There is an element of truth to the thought processes of the addict because a pleasurable euphoria results; however, what goes up must come down, and there is often a leveling out after an addictive high in the form of a depressing low.[1]

Similarly, the desire to escape and avoid pain provides temporary relief and pleasure. When the relief ends, the desire becomes a demand in the mind of the addict who will often stop at nothing to obtain that escape again. The demand for this idolatrous pleasure leads a person into beginning to judge other people. Sinfully judging often involves speculating on others' motives. Most of all, it reveals the absence of a genuine love and concern toward them. When these

---

[1] Sande, Ken, <u>The Peacemaker</u>, Baker Books, Grand Rapids, MI, pp. 102-109.

attitudes are present, our judging has crossed the line and we are playing God.[2] Here is where the behavior of the addict breeds further self-centeredness. ("If you really love me, you, above all people, will help meet my need.") Now, the unmet desire that became a demand becomes a judgmental attitude toward others. As Ken Sande puts it, "Not only have we let an idolatrous desire rule our hearts, but we have also set ourselves up as judging minigods. This is a formula for excruciating conflict."[3]

As you know, an addict who sits in judgment of those who do not help them achieve the idolatrous pleasure has become a horrifically self-centered and difficult person to please. In fact, a loved one cannot please the addict unless they are helping them achieve the pleasure in some way. Some call this "enabling" and it manifests when the addict calls you for money, a ride to the store, or any variety of means intended to get the addict one step closer to the desired pleasure. You become a means to an end, and the relationship becomes contingent upon how much you help them acquire their idol. You cease to be a person anymore to the addict caught in the trap of active addiction, sin, and idolatry.

You feel used by an addict in this state of idolatry, but you don't know what else to do. The addict sees you as object to meet a desire rather than seeing you as a human being with a living soul. In this state, they rarely think of others. An attitude of selfishness is what is most commonly seen in the addict, but the loved one is perplexed and defeated, not knowing what to do.

If a loved one is viewed by the addict as an obstacle to obtaining the idolatrous pleasure they desire, that person will be manipulated, avoided, lied to, or ignored. If a loved one is viewed by the addict as an "enabler" or helper to obtain the idolatrous pleasure, then the loved one will be approached, asked for help, usually in the form of finances, and given "guilt trips" designed to manipulate their emotions. What's left of the relationship between the addict and the loved one is primarily one-sided: "You do for me," says the addict, "and I'll spend some time with you. Otherwise, get out of my way and make no demands upon me in this relationship."

The addict is trapped in the snare of addiction; he or she does not desire a "give and take" relationship with you. Instead, the addict

---

[2] Ibid.
[3] Ibid, p.107.

wants a one-sided relationship: "I take, and you give." Again, the addict sees you as either an obstacle or an "enabler" to get the desired pleasure of choice. Either way, you are viewed as an object and not a person. Alas, many family members, spouses, and friends are willing to have this false relationship with the addict. However, relationships that are this one-sided are doomed to fail, and it will only be a matter of time before you tire of being used by your addicted loved one if you are striving to be healthy in your relationship with Christ.

It is true, however, that some "enablers" (as the world calls it) really like this type of one-sided relationship. The "enabler" will take any type of attention he or she gets from the addict because of the desire for the relationship. Sometimes this desire for an unhealthy relationship is an idolatrous desire in the heart of the family member, spouse, or friend of the addict! While it is a good desire to want a healthy relationship with the addict, the unmet desire for the healthy relationship leads to an unhealthy compromise in which you accept any type of relationship – even one that is destructive to both you and your loved one.

Other "enablers" like being in control (or feeling as if they are in control) of the addict. This is, in its essence, being a "god" to the addict, and yes, it is offensive to Our Holy Creator, God. The addict resents this attitude of the loved one and seeks to avoid pain even more as a result of the unhealthy relationship. This type of "god-like" behavior is often seen in spouses and parents wishing to control their out of control addicts. They mistakenly think they can take responsibility for the addict's behavior (or even control it in some way, such as making the consequences less far-reaching) and it often leads to failure and frustration.

"Enabling" is destructive. "Enabling" means that you are allowing and helping to further the addict's idolatrous practices by your unhealthy, ungodly thinking and actions. Of course, you do not intend to "enable" the addict to keep practicing idolatry because you do want him or her to stop; however, you are caught in this insane cycle of "enabling" the very behaviors you want stopped. You are part of the problem when you are "enabling" an addict to practice idolatry. Now you are committing sin, too.

Why is My Behavior Sinful?

In Ephesians 5:11, the Bible calls Christians to "expose" evil "unfruitful works of darkness." Christians who know that an addict is committing the sin of idolatry cannot allow that relationship to continue by ignoring the seriousness of that offense to God. "Enabling" the sin of idolatry to continue without taking biblical action is also sin, according to Ephesians 5:5-11: **"For you may be sure of this, that everyone who is sexually immoral or impure, or who is covetous (that is, an idolater), has no inheritance in the kingdom of Christ and God. ⁶ Let no one deceive you with empty words, for because of these things the wrath of God comes upon the sons of disobedience. ⁷ Therefore do not associate with them; ⁸ for at one time you were darkness, but now you are light in the Lord. Walk as children of light ⁹ (for the fruit of light is found in all that is good and right and true), ¹⁰ and try to discern what is pleasing to the Lord. ¹¹ Take no part in the unfruitful works of darkness, but instead expose them."⁴**

There is a lot to discuss from this one passage of Scripture, but for now, understand that you are commanded "to discern what is pleasing to the Lord," to "take no part in the unfruitful works of darkness," and to "expose" such unfruitful works according to verses 10-11. If your loved one is caught in the idolatry of addiction, then you must not take part in "enabling" the idolatry to continue. In fact, if your addicted loved one professes to be a Christian, then you are not to have intimate fellowship with such a person who is acting like a hypocrite: **"But now I am writing to you not to associate with anyone who bears the name of brother if he is guilty of sexual immorality or greed, or is an idolater, reviler, drunkard, or swindler—not even to eat with such a one."⁵** A professing Christian is not to act like a drunkard or idolater according to the Scriptures. Therefore, you are to disassociate yourself from such a hypocritical person according to 1 Corinthians 5:13b: **"Purge the evil person from among you."**

How to Stop "Enabling"

You must identify your thoughts and actions that are encouraging and approving (rather than discouraging and disapproving) the idolatrous pleasure-seeking of the addict. Use Appendix A now to

---

4 All Bible verses referenced have been taken from *The Holy Bible:English Standard Version*. 2001 (electronic ed.) . Good News Publishers: Wheaton.
5 1 Corinthians 5:11.

identify those "enabling" thoughts and actions that you are having toward your addicted loved one. To stop "enabling" the addict is not enough. It is half the battle and it is important, but more needs to be done. In the Bible, you are often called to "put off" certain ways of thinking and acting that are sinful and "put on" certain ways of thinking and acting that are righteous and godly. 2 Choices

Use Appendix A to list the ways you are "enabling" your beloved addict, but then for each item you list, write down an opposite "put on" thought and action. For example, if you checked the "put off" item in Appendix A that reads: "After you ask multiple times, I give in and give it to you" then write down a sentence in your own words to "put on." For this item in particular, I would recommend: "After you ask multiple times, I will do what's right in the sight of God and will refuse to give it to you." If you are a parent in this situation and the addict is your son or daughter, you might add: "I will discipline you by _____ if you insist upon asking me after I have told you 'no' the first time."

In Ephesians 5:11, you are to expose those unfruitful works of darkness that the addict is committing like manipulation and lying. If you can identify the guilt, then lovingly confront it. Let the addict know that you see the guilt and hold him or her responsible for it. God holds the addict responsible and so must you. If you catch them in a lie, then expose that lie with the truth. Again, hold the addict accountable just as the Lord does.

Be forewarned. When you begin holding the addict accountable, you will see anger, hurt, resentment, frustration, rage, and bitterness manifest in the addict's demeanor, words, attitudes, and actions toward you. It will happen because they see you as an object, not as a person with emotions, so you should be prepared for it. The addict will act like a three-year old child who gets told "no" when asking for a piece of candy! Expect and plan for an overly dramatic, emotional response and confront them when it happens. It is an attempt to manipulate you.

When you read these words, it may sound pretty disgusting and it is because it is sinful. Reading these words to "stop enabling" the addict sounds easy and straightforward, but as you know, living it out with a real addict with real emotions in a tense, pressure-packed situation is a whole different matter than reading it in a book! Pray before the confrontation that the Holy Spirit will lead you in your attitude, words, and actions because the Lord wants you to become more Christ-like through this experience. He is going to hold you accountable, too, so you want to be sure that you plan ahead so that you can obey Him and successfully persevere through this trial.

Some Final Thoughts on Idolatry

According to Ken Sande, the final stage of idolatry is the punishment phase.[6] He points out that "idols always demand sacrifices. When someone fails to satisfy our demands and expectations, our idol demands that he should suffer. Whether deliberately or unconsciously, we will find ways to hurt or punish people so that they will give in to our desires."[7] The addict may punish you with anger expressed as either a "blow up" or a "clam up."[8] When an addict "blows up," you are punished by experiencing an outburst of angry words, attitudes, or actions. A "blow up" by the addict inflicts pain upon you.

In contrast, a "clam up" occurs frequently with addicts as they withdraw from the relationship with you. A "clam up" punishes you by preventing you from engaging in a meaningful relationship with the addict. A "clam up" also inflicts pain upon the addict as the relationship is often abandoned altogether. An addict who withdraws from you may do so by "acting cool," "withholding affection or physical contact, acting sad or gloomy," and "refusing to look you in the eye."[9]

Either expression of anger (blow up or clam up) is a sinful response toward you and will destroy the relationship if there is not repentance on the part of the addict. If the angry expression toward you is sinful, then you are not allowed to sin in response. The Lord will hold you accountable for your response which must be in total obedience to Him. Yes, you will be hurt and angered by the addict's response, but you are commanded not to sin according to Ephesians 4:26-27: **"Be angry and do not sin; do not let the sun go down on your anger, and give no opportunity to the devil."** You must speak the truth in love[10]

[6] Sande, p. 108-109.
[7] Ibid, p. 108.
[8] Mack, Wayne, A Homework Manual for Biblical Living, Vol. 1 "Personal and Interpersonal Problems," P&R Publishing, Phillipsburg, NJ, p. 10.
[9] Sande, pp. 108-109.
[10] Ephesians 4:15.

to your beloved addict and tell them that their expression of anger to you was sinful, hurtful, and ultimately accountable to the Lord.

This type of responding to an addict may seem so difficult to you primarily because it is so new. It is difficult to realize that you are viewed as simply an object to the addict, but that is the ugly truth. Also, you have bad habit patterns of responding in the past (see your Appendix A checklist) that you must replace with new, improved, and godly responses similar to Christ Jesus in the Gospels. As Jesus experienced in His lifetime on earth, you are experiencing pain and punishment by the addict you love whose heart is being ruled by idolatrous desires. Your suffering is real but it pales in comparison to the suffering that Christ experienced on His way to the Cross and on the Cross.

Romans 12:17 commands you: **"Repay no one evil for evil, but give thought to do what is honorable in the sight of all."** You have to plan ahead in order to deal rightly with this person whom you love with all your heart. Your dealings must be in a manner that pleases God first and "is honorable in the sight of all." It is a very difficult way to live because the emotions, pain, punishment, and rejection you feel are quite strong and real. I repeat, you must plan ahead to do what is right and this book will help you with your planning. Ultimately, you will learn not to take the rejection personally as the idolatrous addict is primarily rejecting God the Father and secondarily rejecting you.

Idolatry is an ugly outward manifestation of a sinful heart. Addiction is rooted in the sinful, idolatrous heart of mankind who seeks to obtain pleasure or avoid pain through a means that provides only momentary fulfillment. Thankfully, Jesus died on the cross to pay the penalty for the sin of idolatry through addiction so the addict can be forgiven by God. If and when he or she is forgiven by God, then you can forgive the addict, too, when that opportunity arises. Until then, pray for the addict to repent and pray that your heart will not be hardened by all of this heinous sin.

Divine Intervention

CHAPTER 2
STEP ONE FOR HELPING AN UNWILLING ADDICT: PRAYER

What do you do when you want your addicted loved one to be clean and sober more than they want it? Pray? Prayer is good but is that all you can do? In some situations, prayer is all that can be done.

For example, on the cross, Jesus prayed for His offenders according to Luke 23:34-38: **"And Jesus said, 'Father, forgive them, for they know not what they do.' And they cast lots to divide his garments. [35] And the people stood by, watching, but the rulers scoffed at him, saying, 'He saved others; let him save himself, if he is the Christ of God, his Chosen One!' [36] The soldiers also mocked him, coming up and offering him sour wine [37] and saying, 'If you are the King of the Jews, save yourself!' [38] There was also an inscription over him, 'This is the King of the Jews.'"**

Rather than allow a sinful "root of bitterness"[11] to spring up in His heart, Jesus prayed to God the Father asking for His offenders to be forgiven. Jesus' compassion for His offenders is reflected in this brief prayer to the Lord: "Father, you forgive them." As a man, Jesus could not give His offenders personal forgiveness. In other words, Jesus as a man could not say, "I forgive you for hurting, mocking, sneering, and killing me." Why could Jesus not forgive in this situation? The answer is that His offenders were not willing to repent for their evil deeds.

In the Bible, you are commanded to forgive others *in your heart* so that bitterness does not take root in your soul. However, what is commonly misunderstood is that you really cannot forgive person to person unless they are first repentant. If you have prayed in your heart for your addicted loved one to repent by turning from the destructive addictive behavior, then it is up to them to repent. You can call the addicted loved one to obedience to Christ by lovingly confronting them. However, unless that person is a born-again Christian, the call to repentance and obedience will be to a Lord and Savior they do not yet serve.

Calls to repentance and obedience are primarily for Christians to return to a right relationship with Christ, and for unbelievers to begin a right relationship with Christ. Therefore, you may need to evangelize your beloved addict until that person becomes a believer in Christ Jesus by the power of the Holy Spirit working through the faithful preaching of

[11] Hebrews 12:15.

the Gospel message contained in the Word of God. Again, radical heart surgery is required prior to seeing any lasting changes in thoughts and behaviors, but God performs that heart surgery. Use Appendix B to help you to share your faith and the Gospel message of hope for the hopeless. Be courageous and share the Good News of Christ Jesus with your addicted loved one today.

Forgiveness Basics

If this teaching on forgiveness is still unclear, let me explain it this way. Imagine that you and your best friend go on a trip and stay in two conjoining rooms at a hotel. Your rooms are separate but next to each other. You have a door in your room that connects to your best friend's room and they have a door as well – one doorway, two doors. When you open your door, what do you see? You see your best friend's door that only he or she can unlock and open. You can knock all day long but unless your best friend decides to open it, you will not be able to go into that room. Your communication and fellowship will be hindered until your best friend opens his or her door.

Your opened door represents your forgiveness. You must be ready and willing to forgive. Your best friend's door represents repentance. Unless your best friend does his or her part by becoming repentant, then your fellowship will be severely hindered. Both doors must be opened for you to have good, eye-to-eye communication, fun and fellowship, and a warm, friendly, deep relationship. Family members must open their door, but true fellowship will not be restored until the addict opens his door of repentance. Family members must be ready and willing to forgive, and not allow bitterness or disappointment in the addict's lack of repentance to harden their heart toward them. Perhaps after many negative consequences, the addict may one day repent.

God wants you to do your part. Pray for the addicted loved one so that your heart doesn't become hardened. Knock on the addicted loved one's door by calling them to repentance and obedience to Christ. Do not let the addict's sinful words or actions "slide by." Confront them by speaking the truth in love[12] and reproving those evil, unfruitful works of darkness.[13] Ignoring the addict's behavior will only make the situation worse in the long run even though the emotional outburst seems worse in the short-term. You must seek to obey and please God, not just please your addicted loved one. Trust God, not your emotions.

---

[12] Ephesians 4:15.
[13] Ephesians 5:11.

CHAPTER 3
THE DIVINE INTERVENTION

Often in secular addiction counseling, an unwilling and unrepentant addict will be confronted by family members, friends, and the addictions counselor in what is called an "intervention." If you have confronted the sinning addict yourself, then you have begun the biblical process of church discipline according to Matthew 18:15-17: **"If your brother sins against you, go and tell him his fault, between you and him alone. If he listens to you, you have gained your brother. [16] But if he does not listen, take one or two others along with you, that every charge may be established by the evidence of two or three witnesses. [17] If he refuses to listen to them, tell it to the church. And if he refuses to listen even to the church, let him be to you as a Gentile and a tax collector."**

The church that follows these biblical principles is a blessing to the Christian and will be a blessing to you. If your church does not follow these biblical commands, but rather sees this teaching of Jesus as "optional," then you may have a problem. Many churches today do not know what to do with Matthew 18:15-20 or are fearful to do anything. God has ordained the church to resolve conflicts when a Christian is committing sins against you. If your addicted loved one is continuing to act rebelliously, irresponsibly, recklessly, or lawlessly toward you and the rules you have established for their own protection, they are sinning against both God and you. The Lord ordained the church to help His people by intervening between two disputing Christians in order to bring peace and resolution to the conflict.

I urge you to search diligently to find a church in your area that desires to honor God by addressing conflicts. If the church is to be concerned with anything, it is to be concerned with reconciling believers in their relationships with one another! You may be fond of your preacher, your choir, your youth groups, your ladies meetings, your softball team, and more, but the most excellent church you can be a part of is one that is interested in reconciling unbelievers to a right relationship with God and reconciling believers to a right relationship with other believers.

Divine Intervention

There are biblical churches doing their best to adhere to these principles in Matthew 18, but they may not be the most alluring or fascinating churches around. Growing believers in Christ will desire a church that will get involved in their problems in a positive way through shepherding, discipleship, and conflict resolution. If you are reading this book, it is most likely that you need the help of the church; it is one resource that the Lord has provided for your help. Ask your church leaders to get involved in your situation. The Lord ordained His church and its leaders to "shepherd" His children according to 1 Peter 5:2-3: **"shepherd the flock of God that is among you, exercising oversight, not under compulsion, but willingly, as God would have you; not for shameful gain, but eagerly; [3] not domineering over those in your charge, but being examples to the flock."** Hopefully, your church takes these verses of the Bible very seriously and will "willingly" get involved in your situation as the Holy Spirit leads them.

After you ask your church for help, you must do what the church asks of you regardless of what you think about it. As a "sheep," you are required to submit to your "shepherding" by the church, so you must follow through with your responsibilities. As long as the church does not tell you to sin, you must obey them and submit to their requests. Do not reject the biblical counsel of your church just because it causes hardship or difficulty.

If your church has no desire to get involved, I am saddened for you, because it is a failure on their part to obey the Lord. By failing God, they are failing you. Again, I urge you to appeal to your pastor and church leaders today to ask them to begin following the biblical principles from Matthew 18:15-20. If they refuse, I would call it sin on their part, and I would urge you to pray and seek out a church that takes this matter of "shepherding" very seriously. It may be that they do not know what to do and if that is the case, then they ought to read this book soon to learn how to deal with an unrepentant or a repentant addict.

If the church refuses to get involved because your addicted loved one has not submitted to the correct and loving counsel and admonition of the church, then that is an entirely different matter. With most addiction cases, unrepentant addicts wear down all of those involved in trying to help them, and your church may be weary of helping at this point. If you and the addict have failed to follow the church's counsel, then you both must repent to the church and ask for their forgiveness prior to beginning the Matthew 18 process again. Not adhering to the church's recommendations makes a church reticent to help, but a repentant attitude by you will go a long way in securing their commitment to get involved again.

Some people think that the church's help has been insufficient because the goal of the family member was to see the addicted loved one repent and be free from the snare of addiction. A church is not able to change the heart of an unrepentant, unwilling, and unbelieving person any more than a secular treatment center is able to change the heart. The Holy Spirit alone, through the ministry of God's Word, changes the heart's desires and thinking into being more biblical and obedient to Christ. If your addicted loved one still suffers from an addiction, it is the addict's fault and not the church.

Specifics in Matthew 18

The church is called by God to follow the principles found in Matthew 18:15-20 for helping its members to obey God. These are not punitive measures, but restorative measures, invented by the Lord and implemented by the church leaders. Since you are dealing with an unrepentant addict, you must follow these biblical truths. When you abide by these truths, you will see how clearly they will define your situation. You will then be more assured of how you must respond to your addicted loved one.

Step One, described by Jesus in verse 15, tells you to go alone to the addicted loved one and "tell him his fault" in private. Likely you have already done this, but if you have not, you must do so now. If the addict listens, then you can begin reading the next section of this book and skip this section! Praise the Lord!

However, if the addict's response is a failure to listen to you, then you must now follow Step Two in Matthew 18:16: "But if he does not listen, take one or two others along with you, that every charge may be established by the evidence of two or three witnesses." Here is where God revealed the "intervention" to us nearly two thousand years ago!

In this biblical intervention, you will take one or two others with you to confront the sinning, selfish addict who professes Christ as Savior. You may take whom you like but I recommend taking at least one representative of your church (a pastor, leader, elder, deacon, or trusted Christian friend) so that the next step if needed will be easier. Again, if the addict listens, then praise the Lord! Go to the next section of this book right now.

However, if the addict fails to listen to this group of people, then you have step three to take, and that is to go to your church leaders (not announcing it to the whole church!). But before we get to step 3, allow me to walk you through some of the details on step 2. When you and one or two others go to confront the addict, open the meeting in prayer. Plan ahead what you would like to say to the addict by writing a letter to read out loud at this meeting. If another family member or trusted friend is there with you at this biblical "intervention," then ask them ahead of time to prepare a short letter or outline to read to the addict as well.

The letter to the addict must first establish an element of love and a desire to have a healthy relationship with the addict. I recommend following the four principles from 2 Timothy 3:16-17: **"All Scripture is breathed out by God and profitable for teaching, for reproof, for correction, and for training in righteousness, [17] that the man of God may be competent, equipped for every good work."**

1. Let your letter contain "teaching" of what a healthy relationship should look like biblically-speaking.
2. Put in a "reproof," or a rebuke, of the addict in your letter. Tell the addict exactly what his or her behavior is doing, how destructive it is to your relationship with them, and how destructive it is to the addict as well. Do not hold back, but be as balanced as you can with the truth spoken in love.
3. Be sure to tell the addict the biblical response that he or she can take to "correct" the problem of addiction. This step is so crucial because it places the responsibility on the addict rather than anywhere else. Do not allow the addict to think that he or she is a victim who is unable to change! That is a lie from Satan that must be replaced with the truth of God's Word.
4. Briefly allude to a plan for change, as this is the disciplined "training in righteousness" required for the addict to really overcome the problem of addiction. You can outline

it some but I would recommend not going into too much depth here.[14] I would state that you will expect regular, weekly attendance at worship services at your church, Bible studies, fellowship meetings with other believers, daily prayer and Bible study, and biblical counseling. You can add other forms of disciplined training as the Holy Spirit leads you. Just be sure they are biblically-based. You may use the sample letter in Appendix C to help you write your own letter.

At this meeting, be sure to present the Good News of the Gospel message. You should have presented the Gospel in the first person-to-person meeting (remember Appendix B?) and you must do so again in this meeting. Either you can present the Gospel or one of the family members, friends, or the pastor (church leader) can do so, but forgiveness for the sins associated with addiction must be emphasized along with the power to change wrought by the Holy Spirit.

If the addict again fails to listen to you, then you will move from Step Two to Step Three, which is to tell the church leaders. Hopefully, the church leaders at your church home will be willing to help you. Few churches actually practice what is known as 'church discipline' but that does not mean you should not ask your church to intervene on your behalf.

Ask your church's pastor and a few of the leaders to meet with you and your addicted loved one. Present your case before them. You can again use your letter from the previous step as an outline to help you bring up the most important sin areas that need to be addressed. Be specific. Mention those areas of sin in which your addicted loved one is failing to uphold his or her God-given responsibilities. Also, mention those sins that the addict is committing like lying, stealing, sexual sin, "drugging" or drinking excessively, and taking illegal drugs. The church leaders must hear all of the evidence so that they will have the best understanding possible.

Then, if your addicted loved one listens to the church leaders and agrees to seek help, praise the Lord for His grace and mercy! If your addicted loved one fails to listen to the church leaders, then they may decide to suspend or excommunicate the addict from membership of

---

[14] You will go into depth spelling out every detail in a later meeting to set up a structured contract.

the church. It is a drastic step to excommunicate someone but it is based on Matthew 18:17 which states to treat the addict as a "Gentile and a tax collector" rather than as a brother or sister in Christ.*

Obviously, no church *wants* to excommunicate a member. However, in obedience to Jesus' words from Matthew 18, an addict who is acting more like an unbeliever, than acting like a believer and disciple of the Lord Jesus Christ needs to be lovingly disciplined by the church and treated as though he or she is an unbeliever. Suspension or dismissal from the church as a member is a "spanking" of sorts by the church and is really a loving action.

The word "excommunication" is so strong in context, that I want to be clear that I am not advocating an attitude of "you are kicked out of the club." Unfortunately, some churches have that mentality of "you are kicked out of the club" and that is not the intention of the Bible in this Matthew 18 passage. The intention of the Word of God is to make your circumstances clear and to make it clear to the sinning addict that this unrepentant attitude is not Christ-like. Therefore, the sinning, unrepentant addict is acting more like a "Gentile and a tax collector" than a Christian. The church must not "wink at sin" because the Lord does not "wink at sin" meaning He does not overlook sin. Unrepentant, unwilling, and unbelieving persons will die and suffer an eternal punishment of hell. Those persons who are repentant, willing, and believing in Christ will die and experience the undeserved and unearned gift of eternal life with God forever in heaven.

The local church is a temporal instrument that the Lord uses to help unrepentant addicts recognize that they are in need of a Savior. Sadly, some churches have rejected the principles of Matthew 18 because it *seems* unloving in their opinion, but they are mistaken. Instead, Matthew 18 is a very loving way to approach addicts who sincerely think they are Christians but are truly not born again. What could be worse than thinking you will be in heaven for all of eternity only to hear what Jesus says in Matthew 7:21-23: **"Not everyone who says to me, 'Lord, Lord,' will enter the kingdom of heaven, but the one who does the will of my Father who is in heaven. 22 On that day many will say to me, 'Lord, Lord, did we not prophesy in your name, and cast out demons in your name, and do many mighty works in your name?' 23 And then will I declare to them, 'I never knew you; depart from me, you workers of lawlessness.'"**

---

* This is not to say the person is forbidden from church attendance - just communing membership.

The desired hope of the type of discipline and rebuke I am referring to here is that the addict will acknowledge that he or she is acting like an unbeliever or admit to being an unbeliever so that the addict can be saved by grace through faith.[15] Your desire ought to be that God give them the fruit of repentance so that they will decide to turn completely away from the sins of addiction.[16]

American culture today discourages the discipline of children and does not embrace this type of discipline by the church, but they are misled. Real love is being a parent who disciplines a child so that the child learns to obey, go to school, and become successful in life. That is parenting on a human level but how does the Heavenly Father parent? Hebrews 12:5-8 tells you: **"And have you forgotten the exhortation that addresses you as sons? 'My son, do not regard lightly the discipline of the Lord, nor be weary when reproved by him. ⁶For the Lord disciplines the one he loves, and chastises every son whom he receives.' ⁷It is for discipline that you have to endure. God is treating you as sons. For what son is there whom his father does not discipline? ⁸If you are left without discipline, in which all have participated, then you are illegitimate children and not sons."**

The Lord's discipline in our lives means He loves us as a caring Father. It is for our own good that God disciplines us and it is for the addict's good that the church be an instrument that the Lord uses to discipline them.

God's Interventions

The Lord has ordained these principles in Matthew 18 for you and your church to follow to bring much needed discipline into your beloved addict's life. The very thing the addict needs is the very thing the addict hates: discipline. The word "discipline" is sometimes viewed by some as a negative word, but it is a positive word since the Bible calls Jesus' followers "disciples." Disciple and discipline have the same English root. They both originate from the same Latin root word, "discipulus" meaning, "pupil." Unfortunately, discipline is not embraced as a good thing by many people who associate "discipline" only with the word, "punishment." Persons in the military recognize

---

[15] Ephesians 2:8-9.

[16] The purpose of this book is not to outline every detail of church discipline. For more on church discipline, please read: <u>Handbook of Church Discipline</u> by Jay E. Adams published by Zondervan.

the serious need for discipline, especially in times of battle, so they embrace the word, "discipline;" however, the average civilian (and addict) does not embrace discipline because of its association in society with punishment.

Hopefully, the addict will repent sometime before the dismissal or excommunication step of the process. If not, then you will have some serious decisions and changes to make. These will be discussed at length in the following chapters. The Lord God, who is the Creator of the heavens, the earth, and everything in the earth, created His "intervention for addiction" thousands of years before the most recent, secular addiction modalities devised their type of "intervention." I know you can trust the Sovereign creator of the universe, God the Father, to give you the wisdom, power, and strength to follow His steps for "intervention" as outlined in the Holy Scriptures.

If not, then are you a Christian? Until this point in the book, I have assumed you are a Christian. If you are not sure, then please read Appendix D and re-examine your relationship with God. You and your addicted loved one can trust God Who is the Creator of the universe. God is Sovereign and capable of doing all of His holy will. Pray for His Will to be done in your life today.

Final Words of Caution

If your family member or loved one is not a professing believer in the Lord Jesus Christ, then church discipline is not an option. The church discipline process is primarily designed to protect, help, and serve members of the body of Christ; therefore, if they are not a member of the local church, then church discipline is not applicable. This does not mean that you cannot ask your pastor, church leaders, and trusted Christian friends for help to intervene in your situation, because one of the functions of the church is to share the good news of the saving grace of the Gospel message with unbelievers.[17] The authority of the church only extends to believing members of its denomination.[18]

---

[17] Matthew 28:18-20.

[18] Note: Church discipline is practiced regularly in most PCA Presbyterian churches but it may be a foreign concept to your church. There are legal aspects to consider in today's litigious society so I suggest you speak to an attorney before making public any church discipline matters. Really, most church discipline matters

Now, if you are dealing with an unbeliever, then there is another "divine intervention" ordained by the Lord to protect, help, and serve you: the government. The majority of lawmakers and law enforcers in society are employed by the government and given the authority by God to protect all people of that community. Even if your addicted loved one is a close relative whom you love very much, you still have an obligation to society to protect the community from someone who is acting rebelliously and lawlessly. You are to think of others more highly than you think of yourself. What if he or she leaves your home under the influence of narcotics and has a car wreck killing the mother of two small children? Would you experience guilt knowing that he or she acted recklessly and the actions resulted in two young children losing their mother?

God instructed His people to think about the community more than themselves in Deuteronomy 21:18-21: **"¹⁸ If a man has a stubborn and rebellious son who will not obey the voice of his father or the voice of his mother, and, though they discipline him, will not listen to them, ¹⁹ then his father and his mother shall take hold of him and bring him out to the elders of his city at the gate of the place where he lives, ²⁰ and they shall say to the elders of his city, 'This our son is stubborn and rebellious; he will not obey our voice; he is a glutton and a drunkard.' ²¹ Then all the men of the city shall stone him to death with stones. So you shall purge the evil from your midst, and all Israel shall hear, and fear."**

These are stunning words. What God was stating in this passage to Israel is that a rebellious, gluttonous, drunken child who is failing to listen to the loving discipline of parents is to be turned over to the authorities, or the "elders of his city," for punishment. Despite modern society's attempts to equate "punishment" and "discipline" based upon some similarities between the words, they are really two different words.

The word "punish" has a Latin association to pain and penalty. In punishment, one is exacting a punitive measure as a penalty for a violation of a code, rule, or law so that the violation does not occur again for the betterment of society. Punishment is *always* designed to hurt. Discipline is different, however, as it is associated with learning and teaching a "pupil." While discipline may "hurt" or

---

should remain private and only involve those necessarily concerned. For more on church discipline, read Jay Adams' book, <u>Handbook of Church Discipline</u>.

be "uncomfortable" at times, it is designed to be instructive and is not necessarily painful to a person. Discipline may be structured, rigorous, and demanding but when faithfully and diligently followed, it is not necessarily painful to the pupil.

An easy way for Christians to think about the difference between discipline and punishment is in relation to God their Father. For example, Christians saved by grace through faith will NEVER be punished by God or experience His divine justice and wrath toward sin. Jesus suffered that punishment for the Christian who deserved to receive the punishment but will not. Instead, Christians saved by grace through faith will ALWAYS experience discipline and chastening by God the Father (Hebrews 12:7-11) as a good parent who desires to instruct, teach, and protect His son or daughter from harm. Discipline may be painful at times but it does not *have* to be painful. Discipline may be structured in such a way that the learner never experiences pain.

God has ordained the church to discipline His people out of love and concern for them. God has given the church authority to lovingly discipline His people to protect them from the harmful effects of sin. When God's people sin, they experience pain and suffering. It grieves our loving Father to watch His children choose to sin because they are choosing to inflict needless suffering upon themselves. Do not view church discipline as "punishment" because it is certainly not punitive. It can be painful for the unwilling, unrepentant addict but it will be instructive and fruitful for the willing, repentant addict to bring them closer to a loving Father.

God has ordained the government to punish lawbreakers, and His people are included in that punishment when they violate society's laws. God does not give His children a "get out of jail free card" so why should you give your addicted loved one a "get out of jail free card" when he/she breaks the established laws of the land? You should not give your addicted loved one a "free pass" to sin. To do so would be wrong even if he or she is your son or daughter. You have an obligation to the community to help promote peace and unity regardless if the lawbreaker is related to you or loved by you. Do what is right in the eyes of God as Colossians 3:23-24 states: **"Whatever you do, work heartily, as for the Lord and not for men, [24] knowing that from the Lord you will receive the inheritance as your reward. You are serving the Lord Christ."**

CHAPTER 4
AN UNREPENTANT, PRODIGAL SON

You have now reached an unfortunate portion and probably the most difficult chapter of this book: what to do with an unwilling, unrepentant addict. This addict is acting like an unbeliever who does not love the Lord Jesus Christ. It is sad that it has come to this moment where you are questioning the very salvation of your addicted loved one. Is the addict a believer or not? This is a tough question to answer because you cannot look into his or her heart; however, you can judge by the fruit of the addict's actions.

Judging by the fruit, is this person acting like someone who loves Christ? Jesus said in John 13:34-35, **"A new commandment I give to you, that you love one another: just as I have loved you, you also are to love one another. ³⁵ By this all people will know that you are my disciples, if you have love for one another."** How will people know that you and I are Jesus' disciples? The answer is in verse 35 above: when "you have love for one another."

Therefore, ask yourself: is my addicted loved one acting in a manner that demonstrates love for me and others? You know the answer to that question if you have reached the dismissal or excommunication step of the Matthew 18 process. No, your addicted loved one is acting as though he or she is an unbeliever. It is a very sad and profound realization.

On the other hand, now you know how to pray and what to do. You must pray that the Lord will send people to share the Gospel with your addicted loved one, and you must seize any opportunity to share the Good News of the Gospel message with him or her. Apart from a real, personal, and dynamic relationship with the Lord Jesus Christ, there is no hope for the addict. For this reason, share the Gospel and pray that God will send people to the addict in order to lead the addict to the Lord Jesus.

The Lost Son

In Luke 15, Jesus told one of His most famous parables. Some call it the parable of the "prodigal" son while others call it the parable of the "lost" son. Here is this parable in its entirety. While you may have read and studied this before, you may be surprised at some of the applications of this parable for your circumstances. I encourage you to read Luke 15:11-32 slowly once and then read it again before reading further in this book.

> And he said, "There was a man who had two sons. [12] And the younger of them said to his father, 'Father, give me the share of property that is coming to me.' And he divided his property between them. [13] Not many days later, the younger son gathered all he had and took a journey into a far country, and there he squandered his property in reckless living. [14] And when he had spent everything, a severe famine arose in that country, and he began to be in need. [15] So he went and hired himself out to one of the citizens of that country, who sent him into his fields to feed pigs. [16] And he was longing to be fed with the pods that the pigs ate, and no one gave him anything.
>
> [17] "But when he came to himself, he said, 'How many of my father's hired servants have more than enough bread, but I perish here with hunger! [18] I will arise and go to my father, and I will say to him, "Father, I have sinned against heaven and before you. [19] I am no longer worthy to be called your son. Treat me as one of your hired servants."' [20] And he arose and came to his father. But while he was still a long way off, his father saw him and felt compassion, and ran and embraced him and kissed him. [21] And the son said to him, 'Father, I have sinned against heaven and before you. I am no longer worthy to be called your son.' [22] But the father said to his servants, 'Bring quickly the best robe, and put it on him, and put a ring on his hand, and shoes on his feet. [23] And bring the fattened calf and kill it, and let us eat and celebrate. [24] For this my son was dead, and is alive again; he was lost, and is found.' And they began to celebrate.

²⁵ "Now his older son was in the field, and as he came and drew near to the house, he heard music and dancing. ²⁶ And he called one of the servants and asked what these things meant. ²⁷ And he said to him, 'Your brother has come, and your father has killed the fattened calf, because he has received him back safe and sound.' ²⁸ But he was angry and refused to go in. His father came out and entreated him, ²⁹ but he answered his father, 'Look, these many years I have served you, and I never disobeyed your command, yet you never gave me a young goat that I might celebrate with my friends. ³⁰ But when this son of yours came, who has devoured your property with prostitutes, you killed the fattened calf for him!' ³¹ And he said to him, 'Son, you are always with me, and all that is mine is yours. ³² It was fitting to celebrate and be glad, for this your brother was dead, and is alive; he was lost, and is found.' "

Now, let's take a closer look at a few of the elements in this parable that can be applied to your situation. A word of caution, however, is that one must be careful with the parables that Jesus taught in the Scriptures because they were illustrations, and some details mentioned are for illustrative purposes rather than to be taken literally. Nonetheless, as we look deeper into this parable, you will learn more about how to handle your situation with your addicted loved one.

In this parable, Jesus painted a picture of an "extreme sinner" in the younger son who basically says, "Dad, I wish you were dead so I could have my inheritance. In fact, give me my inheritance now. I do not desire to have a relationship with you." This younger son sees his father as an object. Is this the picture of your addicted loved one who is trapped in active addiction? The addict tells you he does not love you, asks you for money, or tells you that he wishes you were dead so you cannot stop him from getting what he wants. Sound familiar? You are an obstacle to the addict. The selfishness of addiction is very ugly when it gets to this stage.

The father in this parable represents God the Father, but there are some things you can learn to emulate from the father in this parable.

Divine Intervention

First, the father let the son go. When the younger son got so bold as to say these things to his own father, the parent let his son go. Maybe you are in a situation where you have reached the end of anything productive with your beloved addict. If the relationship has soured to this point, then there really is no real relationship left.

If you are to this point with your beloved addict, then the loving action often is letting them go. Does this sound harsh? It may be the most difficult thing you have ever had to do, but you must cover it in prayer and trust God to work in your situation. Really, what else can you do when someone is acting so hatefully against you and all you are trying to do is to help them? You can see how twisted the addicted mind gets. The very person who is able to help and who desires to help is the very person the addict rejects. Now, by experience, you have a glimpse of what the Lord God experiences when people reject Him.

If your addicted loved one will not leave voluntarily but would prefer to stay, disrespect you, scoff at your rules, and use your money to finance an addiction, then you have a biblical leg to stand on from Proverbs 22:10 in telling the addict to leave your home: **"Drive out a scoffer, and strife will go out, and quarreling and abuse will cease."** Notice the words "drive out" are not telling you to "ask politely." Many have had to "drive out a scoffer" who refused to follow the rules of the home but wanted the benefits of living in the home. The primary motivation for an addict in this state of mind is that he or she can avoid paying rent and other bills in order to work and spend money on the addiction. The addict in this scenario has "got it made" and you will have to drive the addict out.

Nonetheless, the younger son in this parable left voluntarily. Some addicts will also leave voluntarily because they desire to get as far away as possible from those people who love them and are telling them "no." The younger son took his money and took a "journey into a far country, and there he squandered his property in reckless living." You can imagine what the addict did to squander his property: drugs, alcohol, prostitution, gambling, shopping for extravagant clothes, homosexual prostitution, and more. Those temporary pleasures do not last long because the addict in this state does not have unlimited resources. The younger son "spent everything" he had; your beloved addict will do the same.

Here's a problem, however. Often, an addict will attach himself to someone he can use for financial gain. Female addicts do the same thing: attach themselves to someone who can take care of their financial needs. It is very common. Addicts have a "self-first mentality" called selfishness. But isn't it odd that an addict will put up with the restrictions, rules, pain, abuse, and aggravation of someone he or she has made the choice to attach themselves to, yet *refuse* to live under your restrictions, rules, and 'aggravation'? Don't you find that to be ironic?

Addicts want to use and they do not want the reminder of guilt from you that they are failing in their responsibilities. Therefore, the addict leaves for a "far country" and attaches to someone else. The younger son did this very same thing in verse 15. The verse says "hired himself out to one of the citizens" but the implications here from the original Greek language is that he has attached himself to this citizen for financial support. The citizen sends him off to feed the pigs, and "no one gave him anything." Even this attached relationship with the citizen has failed for the addict who now longs to eat what the pigs are eating.

One more aspect to bring out is a phrase from verse 14: "a severe famine arose in that country, and he began to be in need." What this famine means to you is that the people of that day did not have any extra material resources to give to anyone else. People needed everything they owned for their very own survival. No one had extra to give this "leach" – the younger, prodigal son.

Here is an important lesson. When the addict has no one from whom to "mooch" for finances, he or she begins to be "in need." You must cut off the addict's financial resources and pray that others will grow weary of supporting your lazy, selfish, and addicted loved one. Talk to your extended family members to tell them they do NOT need to give your addicted loved one any form of financial support: money, housing, clothing, and even food. You do not have to tell them "why" but you can tell them to trust you because they will know that you love the addict.

Not giving them food may sound harsh but look at this parable again. Verse 16 states "he was longing to be fed with the pods that the pigs ate" so it was a real, physiological need that was not being met that led the younger son to repent in the next verses. In modern language, the word "need" is misused as it usually refers to a "desire." "I need that expensive new car" should be restated as "I desire that expensive new car." Real needs are food, clothing, and shelter.

Your addicted loved one must be in real need before real change is sought. As long as you allow the addicted loved one to live in your house, eat your food, drive your car, and wear clothes you have purchased, they will not leave. Maybe that is really what you want deep down inside. Is it? Are you afraid that your addicted loved one may leave and die resulting in thoughts and feelings of guilt in your heart? Are you afraid your addicted loved one will leave and reject you? Do you want to control them and pretend you are god? Can you really protect the addict from the harmful consequences of the addiction anyway?

These are tough questions you need to ask yourself. The truth is that addicts will always stay addicted if they never experience any temporal, painful consequences. Is that what you want: the addict not to experience pain and thereby not change? I hope not if you are a Christian, because the addict is destroying his or her purpose in Christ, relationship with God the Father, and every significant and healthy human relationship. Active addiction is not what is best for your loved one.

Modeling the Father

What should you do? Ephesians 5:1 states: **"Therefore be imitators of God, as beloved children."** Of course, you must pray and ask the Lord to lead you by the Holy Spirit whenever you do implement some of these difficult stances with your addicted loved one. That is not an option. The Lord wants you to imitate Him and you have a model Person who reveals God the Father in the Gospels: Jesus.

In this parable, Jesus tells that the father let his son go. The father gave the son his inheritance, which would have been a cultural disgrace in that day and time, but the father acted lovingly to the son. Likewise, you can tell the addict to leave, make arrangements for them to have a place to live, a car, groceries, and clothing if you like, but do not co-sign your name to anything.

Take your name off of any bank accounts, cars, and the like because the addict will squander it all when continuing in active addiction. There is no reason to think they are going to change simply because you made them leave. Quite the opposite is true. The addict is now "free" to fulfill the lusts of the flesh even more. However, the responsibilities of life will catch up to them eventually, and the addict will be back to ask you for more money or financial support. Count on it.

After you let the addict go or drive them out, your strife and quarrelling will cease[19] *if* you model the father in this parable. The father did not chase down the addict, "Son, come back." The father did not text message the son everyday. The father did not call the son on the cell phone to tell him that he loved him. The father let him go. The relationship ended. The father did not choose to end the relationship; his son did. The father was looking for the son to return in verse 20: **"but while he was still a long way off, his father saw him and felt compassion."** Never give up praying for your addicted loved one because your relationship with God must not end even though your relationship with the addict has ended temporarily.

There will be many things that the Lord will teach you during this time of not communicating with your addicted loved one. You must turn to God in prayer and Bible study and continue to trust Him. The Lord wants you to grow more Christ-like through this trial and the only way you can fail is by failing to please God. If you disobey Him, then you have failed. If you obey Him, there will be blessings in store for you down the road although you must not be motivated only by receiving blessings.

Remember, the father "ran and embraced him and kissed him". Fervent prayer will help prevent your heart from hardening against your addicted loved one. Yes, you have been deeply hurt and offended by the words and actions of the addict, but remember that the addict is first of all rebelling against the Lord, and not you. You are secondarily offended and the Lord is primarily offended by the actions of the addict because it is a sin issue. There is forgiveness available for the addict through the blood of Jesus, and it is the addict who must repent. There is no way around it.

The Son's Repentance

In this parable, the younger son came to his senses, repented, and realized how loving and caring his father had been to him and even the "hired servants" (v. 17). It was the younger son's remembrance of

---

[19] Proverbs 22:10.

the father's love that woke him up from his debauchery. The addict you love knows that you love them. The Lord's lasting, "agape" love, however, is what you must desire for the addict to know and that's why sharing the Gospel is so critical.

When the addict wakes up by coming to his senses, it is the Heavenly Father's love that will cause them to return to a right relationship with the Father and with you. You are in a situation where you are totally dependent upon the grace of God to intervene with His infinite wisdom and love. Until the addict repents, there is very little you can do.

The good news is that the younger son in this parable did repent according to verses 18-21. Here's what repentance sounds like in verse 18: "I have sinned against heaven and before you. I am no longer worthy to be called your son (or daughter or husband or wife or grandchild or friend or whatever)." Wouldn't you like to hear those words from your addicted loved one today?

These words are the words of a repentant heart because they take responsibility for sin. No one else is to blame when the addict says, "I have sinned against heaven and before you." The addict blames himself and takes responsibility; this is what is required in order for the addict to be transformed by the renewal of the mind. In fact, it is evidence of it.[20] As you can tell, the younger son in the parable has had a complete change of mind from living in the pride and selfishness of addiction, and he is now *willing* to be reconciled to the one who truly loves him.

The attitude of the son is much different than it was earlier in this parable. The younger son is not coming back to his father saying, "Hey, Old man, I'm back. Did you miss me? I'm sorry for the way I acted before. Can I move back in and take your car out with my buddies tonight? I promise I'll do better this time. Oh, by the way, can I borrow twenty bucks, too?" No!!! That was not this younger son's attitude at all! It was an attitude of repentance.

When your addicted loved one finally comes to repentance, you will know it. There will be a distinct difference between the person you used to see enslaved to an addiction and the person you now see who is willing to do anything just to begin repairing the relationship with you. The younger son said in verse 19, "I am not worthy to be called

---

[20] Romans 12:2.

your son. Treat me as one of your hired servants" indicating a heart of humility and repentance. He recognized that he had 1) not acted as a good son, 2) asked for his inheritance so he could be free from any familial obligations, and 3) left his family for a life of luxurious living. He did not deserve to be a son again and that was reflected by these statements in verse 19.

In verse 21, the father did not allow the son to say "treat me as one of your hired servants" which was different from the son's planned speech in verse 19. The father restored the relationship with his son, and so must you if your addicted loved one repents. Again, repentance is a big deal to God and that type of repentant heart will be very evident to you. You will see less selfishness, pride, anger, depression, and other detrimental attitudes. Repentance like this younger son's repentance is tangible. You can measure it, observe it, and see it because it is not fake. The father was ready and willing to reconcile with his son. Are you?

The Older Son's Sinful Response

What is so disappointing in this parable is the response of the older brother! Jesus actually told this parable to the Pharisees because of their legalistic, self-righteous attitude toward repentant sinners. You must not allow yourself to be like a Pharisee if your loved one repents. You must guard against this mindset because it so easy to think this way. Many non-addicted persons think this way and you may see this type of self-righteous attitude by others in your family when the addict repents. It is unfortunate but often true. Those self-righteous family members and friends need to be reminded about the goodness and forgiveness of God toward repentant sinners who recognize their need for a Savior.

The father was so happy that he threw a huge party for his son. Likewise, you need to celebrate the repentance of your addicted loved one because this is a special act of Christ. Repentance is granted by God. 2 Timothy 2:24-26 states: **"And the Lord's servant must not be quarrelsome but kind to everyone, able to teach, patiently enduring evil, [25] correcting his opponents with gentleness. <u>God may perhaps grant them repentance</u> leading to a knowledge of the truth, [26] and they may escape from the snare of the devil, after being captured by him to do his will** (emphasis mine)." If God has granted repentance and the addict has escaped from the snare of the devil, then it is time to celebrate!

Final Thoughts and Words of Caution

This parable taught by Jesus was designed to illustrate a point to the Pharisees about sin, repentance, forgiveness, and God's grace. While we do not want to read too much into this parable, it is important to note that the time frame from when the younger son left with his inheritance and came back to the father is unknown. The father is obviously very wealthy so the inheritance was probably substantial which means that it may have been a long period of time before the younger son squandered all of it. Then the younger son "began to be in need" (v.14) but he did not repent right away. Instead, he attached himself to a citizen of that country (v.15) which means he was still trying to fix the situation in his own strength rather than repenting and turning to God. At this point, he was still suffering and struggling with his sinful heart until repentance came in verse 17.

This shows that you may have to wait a very long time before your loved one repents and turns to God. You will have to continue to pray, read your Bible, and trust God for the outcome until repentance happens, but you must let your addicted loved one go. You are not God and cannot control this situation in the least bit. Calling the addict everyday, sending money, and trying to keep some semblance of a relationship together when the addict is unwilling, unrepentant, hateful, prideful, and selfish will not work. You cannot change the addict's heart.

The addict will come back, as the Prodigal Son did, if and when he begins to be in a state of real, physiological need causing him to "come to himself" and repent just as this younger son did. Some counselors recommend that unwilling addicts attend "treatment" or "rehabilitation" centers to give them the opportunity to change. I do not. I recommend jail for unwilling addicts who are breaking the laws of mankind. I recommend real consequences rather than giving an addict a "treatment" experience costing thousands of dollars that merely postpones the inevitable. If the addict is unwilling, no "treatment" or "rehabilitation" center in the world will change his heart so the "treatment" experience becomes a delay in the plans of the addict to return to active addiction.

The addict must experience the devastating consequences of addiction such as jail, hunger, and homelessness that often lead to the final consequence: death. Many addicts die from their excessive indulgences in the addiction. It is very sad. Because you know that addicts die, you may be thinking you can prevent the addict from dying, if you "at least allow my addicted loved one to live with me." You cannot prevent the addict from indulging or dying. The relationship you have with the addict is nearly dead because that person views you as an object rather than as a real person who loves him or her.

Let the addict go. Quit spending money and wasting time on "rehabilitation" programs that teach humanistic, selfish, and man-centered ideas to an already selfish, self-centered addict. When the addict leaves "treatment," you will have a bigger monster on your hands even if the addict is now temporarily "clean and sober." Now he or she is clean, self-righteous, with a "disease" label on which to blame their behavior. They can even blame God for giving them the disease! In fact, his parents are to blame, too, for his addictive choices! Can you see how happy you have made the addict now?

Let me add a positive hope in favor of some treatment programs. Christian treatment programs that are truly biblically based may be preferred to living with someone. However, these are few and far between. Teen Challenge* is one I recommend because they have a high success rate and emphasize repentance and responsibility, and they depend on God's intervention in the life of the addict. The best case scenario is to encourage a relationship to develop between the addict and someone else (same sex) in a real-life setting because so many people who go to treatment return to the same environment (problems) and go right back to using. Treatment programs tend to be a safe, sterile, yet unrealistic environment, but for meth and some other drugs, it may be unavoidable and needed.

Often, it is only a short amount of time before the unwilling addict who finished "treatment" and is now "clean and sober" returns to active addiction. The addiction may be different now but it will be just as destructive. Do not think that sending an unwilling addict to "treatment" or "rehab" will cause lasting, heart change in their life. The addict needs heart surgery from the Lord that most often comes

---

* Teen Challenge is now a residential program for adults, not teens but they kept the name.

by experiencing hard, negative consequences. You must trust and wait upon the Lord to do His heart surgery on them. **"The LORD is good to those who wait for him, to the soul who seeks him. [26] It is good that one should wait quietly for the salvation of the LORD"** (Lamentations 3:25-26).

This chapter must end just as it began. This is a very sad and profound realization. Your loved one may die, never having repented and trusted in the Lord for eternal life. He or she may spend eternity in everlasting torment - a conscious, excruciatingly painful punishment reserved for those unrepentant unbelievers who reject God's free gift of salvation and forgiveness from their sins. The following prayer example must be your heart's cry:

"God of heaven and earth, Who made the seas and the land and everything in them, I ask You in Your mercy to send Your faithful people to accurately and passionately share the good news of Jesus Christ and His salvation freely offered to my loved one _____. Cause me to seize any and every opportunity to share the gospel message with him/her also. I realize that apart from a real and personal relationship with You, through Jesus Christ, there is no hope for _____. Your will be done.

Amen.

SECTION 2
WILLING AND REPENTANT ADDICTS

Divine Intervention

CHAPTER 5
THE HARD WORK BEGINS

If you are reading this section of the book, then the good news is that you have a willing and repentant loved one you can help to overcome their addiction. I rejoice with you and hope that this is truly the case. You will see if it is real repentance once you begin to implement the strategies outlined in this section of the book. You will know if there is true repentance because the addict's words and actions will reflect a very different heart attitude than before. Do not expect them to be perfect and never to sin again because that will not happen.

Some addicts fake a repentant attitude and seem zealous for the Lord when really they are just buying time. For this reason, you must judge the fruit of the addict: their words and actions. Words and actions must match. Good words followed by bad actions equals unrepentance. Do not be fooled by mere words. Talk is cheap.

The three heart attitudes that you want to look for in the addict's words and actions are *responsibility, gratitude,* and *submission.* If any one of these three elements is missing, you may not have true sorrow that leads to repentance without regret. 2 Corinthians 7:10 says: **"For godly grief (sorrow) produces a repentance that leads to salvation without regret, whereas worldly grief (sorrow) produces death** (word change mine)." There are two types of grief and sorrow: godly and worldly. The addict, who is not willing to submit to you, who grumbles and complains often, or who fails to take responsibility for actions is probably not experiencing godly sorrow but worldly sorrow. Worldly sorrow says, "I'm sorry I got caught. I'm not sorry I committed the sin." If there is godly grief and sorrow, repentance will manifest without any regrets from the addict according to 2 Corinthians 7:10, and the repentant words, thoughts, and actions will be clear to you in time.

"But Doesn't the Addict NEED Treatment?"

At this point in the process of helping a willing addict, many people recommend sending the repentant addict off to a "treatment" or "rehabilitation" center for help. In most cases, I do not.[21] A few people are indeed helped by spending time in "treatment" or "rehabilitation." Understand, however, that "treatment and rehabilitation" is a big business industry and people spend billions of dollars each year on attempts at "treatment." I hear many reports of "treatment" damaging family situations and costing thousands of dollars in the process.

One more warning about "treatment" centers is that "treatment" is designed to change the thinking of the addict – which, I agree, is essential for real change. However, I have a problem with how the majority of "treatment" centers change a person's thinking, because they do so in a man-centered way – devoid of God and biblical teachings. This is problematic from a Christian standpoint. A self-centered man or woman who is no longer addicted to one thing often switches the addiction to another temporary pleasure.[22] It is a vicious cycle and human-centered teachings are lacking in too many aspects to go into detail here. For now, understand that sending the willing, Christian addict off to "treatment" may do more harm than good.

Transformation without Treatment

The Romans 12:2 transformation process begins in the brain of the addict. The addict's thinking must be changed before the habitual behaviors will change. There is no other way around it. In this regard, treatment centers are starting at the right place: the brain and its thinking. However, God requires the Christian to not be conformed to the worldly, man-centered (or human-centered) way of thinking in Romans 12:2: **"Do not be conformed to this world, but be transformed by the renewal of your mind, that by testing you may discern what is the will of God, what is good and acceptable and perfect."**

God's will is not that your loved one *just* remain clean and sober but that he or she has victory by accomplishing His will. The goal is learning to please God in thought, word, and deed. No one can please God without the renewing of the mind by His Word and by the power of the Holy Spirit. The addict will not have a mind renewal until his or her thinking begins to line up with the Lord's thinking as revealed

---

[21] Methamphetamine addiction is so physiologically powerful that I do recommend sending people to a residential program (biblically-based preferred) for help with that specific addiction. The only place I can 100% recommend with a clear conscience is "His Steps Ministries" in Atlanta, GA, with Mr. Tim Brown. Meth addicts require residential settings.

[22] The switch is very often to sexual acts of pleasure.

in His Word. For this reason, "treatment" centers may help a person to clean up from the addictive behaviors, but frequently this will not be a lasting change because there are few biblical principles taught in "treatment."

The biblical alternative to "treatment" is that the addict must live with and be discipled by a mature Christian who will serve to disciple the addict. Jesus not only taught His disciples but He lived with them. They watched Him and learned how He interacted, loved, and dealt with people. They modeled Him. Likewise, an important piece of discipleship is this component of modeling. The addict needs a wise Christian to model within the context of a restrictive living environment.[23]

No one is perfect so there will be aspects of the more mature Christian that should not be modeled of course. Nevertheless, the addict can learn to change best from being around this Christian person full-time. Can the addict work a job? Yes. Can the addict give this person some space? Yes. Is this type of commitment inconvenient for the more mature Christian? Yes. This type of commitment really demonstrates a selfless, Christ-like attitude to the addict and it is essential for discipleship.

The sins associated with addiction are life-devastating and life-dominating sin, and are not easily overcome. It takes a huge commitment from the addict and from a more mature Christian, but it is better to accomplish it this way than to send the person to "treatment." If the commitment is three months, find out how much "treatment" costs and pay this more mature Christian for the sacrifice given. You would pay this amount for "treatment" anyway so why not financially bless one of God's children who is sacrificing for the addict's benefit?

I really wish more persons were willing to serve as a discipler who would allow this kind of person into their home. This method has been effective numerous times and is the biblical way. What is a month or two of inconvenienced living compared to a soul saved and sanctified? If you are a Christian, you know the answer. Many Christians who used to be enslaved to a physical addiction tell me that they were changed by living with a more mature Christian in a discipleship relationship.

I recommend that you find someone who has no relation or family connections with the addict if at all possible. That is not always possible so a distant relative would be the next best choice. If neither of these

---

[23] The restrictive living environment will be addressed later in the next chapter.

two options is available, then you are the next best option. Be sure that whoever takes on this commitment is a mature Christian. Also, be sure the addict understands the sacrifice of this person and that the addict is being shown the love of Christ in a very practical and real way.

I recommend that the two of them go everywhere (within reason) together. Do things together as much as possible. These opportunities allow the addict the opportunity to see the mature Christian live out his or her faith in front of the addict just as Christ did in front of His disciples. It is imperative that the mature Christian and the addict be of the same sex.

This manner of discipleship may surprise you because you live in a day where everyone "refers out" to "experts" for help. However, you will be surprised at how powerful this live-in relationship of discipleship will be for the addict and the discipler. It will change both of their lives. Again, I have witnessed several transformations as a result of this type of relational discipleship.

Transforming by Truth

The transformation process of addictive thinking and behaving takes a lifetime. You will have ups and downs, but the good news is that eventually there will be more ups than downs. In the meantime, you will need to be strong in the Lord and courageous in implementing a plan for change. The change that the Lord wants to see in the addict is Christ-likeness. It is called "progressive sanctification" in the church and it will never be achieved perfectly here on earth. However, there will be signs of Christ-likeness in the form of humility, less self-centeredness, and a much more giving attitude. You will see the addict become more responsible, grateful, and submissive.

It is a transformation process of becoming like Christ – not a recovery process. The goals are different. You will see some of the fruit of the Spirit: love, joy, peace, patience, kindness, goodness, faithfulness, gentleness, and self-control[24] manifest more frequently. Again, the three things I really look for are responsibility, gratitude, and a submissive spirit. If those things are being evidenced, then you likely have a repentant addict who is ready and willing to change into Christ-likeness.[25]

---

[24] Galatians 5:22-23.
[25] For more on what to look for, read the book, The Heart of Addiction by Mark E. Shaw

Discipleship

A plan for change is not punishment. It is discipline and there is a difference. Punishment is the infliction of a penalty for wrongdoing. In His justice, God had to punish the sins of mankind. God could not "wink" at sin by letting it go unpunished. Sin came into the world by one man (Adam) according to 1 Corinthians 15:21-22: **"For as by a man came death, by a man has come also the resurrection of the dead. For as in Adam all die, so also in Christ shall all be made alive."** The good news is that by one man (Jesus) all of mankind can be saved because the Lord punished the sins of mankind through Jesus' death on the cross.

Discipline is different from punishment. Discipline is defined as "training that corrects, molds, or perfects the mental faculties or moral character."[26] Biblically, it is training with a purpose. Disciples are under the discipline of their teacher. Disciples of Christ are under the discipline of Christ. All Christians are disciples of Christ by the work of the Holy Spirit as they are being trained, taught, sanctified, molded, and perfected into the "mental faculties and moral character" of Jesus Christ. Christians are to become like Christ in thoughts, words, and actions.

Discipline may mean that a disciple cannot do what he or she always wants to do. It may not always be fun but it will be beneficial to the disciple long-term. Addicts have a hard time accepting discipline and often view it as punishment. Addicts need discipline. They need restrictions. When they violate those restrictions, they need to be disciplined by experiencing pre-determined consequences.

For example, I strongly recommend that you and the addict sit down with the discipler to lay out a detailed, practical plan for change. If the addict is adhering to the stipulations of a specific plan for change or contract, then go ahead and pre-determine the consequences for violating the contract. Therefore, when the violation occurs (and it will occur), determine the consequence ahead of time so that the addict is aware of it. Then when the violation occurs, you will enforce the consequence without it being personal, unplanned, or emotionally charged. Follow through and do not allow the consequence to slide. Chances are that one of the reasons the addict got involved so heavily with an addiction is that he or she "slid" by not receiving the proper discipline at the appropriate time in the past.

---

[26] Merriam-Webster, Inc. *Merriam-Webster's Collegiate Dictionary.* Includes index. 10th ed. Springfield, Mass., U.S.A.: Merriam-Webster, 1996, c1993.

Divine Intervention

Some define discipline as a punishment for the sake of discipline. While that is an acceptable definition, I really stress the idea of discipline as "good" and punishment as "bad" because there was only one punishment for all time for Christians! God punished His own Son for our sins! It is amazing love indeed.

The Lord's discipline of His children is on-going and discipline is training. It is necessary for making His children more like Christ in every possible way. Use the word "discipline" rather than "punishment" when you deal with your addict. Use the word "discipleship" for what you and others will be doing to help the addict become Christ-like. Remember Hebrews 12:5-11 states:

> "And have you forgotten the exhortation that addresses you as sons? 'My son, do not regard lightly the discipline of the Lord, nor be weary when reproved by him. [6] For the Lord disciplines the one he loves, and chastises every son whom he receives.' [7] It is for discipline that you have to endure. God is treating you as sons. For what son is there whom his father does not discipline? [8] If you are left without discipline, in which all have participated, then you are illegitimate children and not sons. [9] Besides this, we have had earthly fathers who disciplined us and we respected them. Shall we not much more be subject to the Father of spirits and live? [10] For they disciplined us for a short time as it seemed best to them, but he disciplines us for our good, that we may share his holiness. [11] For the moment all discipline seems painful rather than pleasant, but later it yields the peaceful fruit of righteousness to those who have been trained by it."

CHAPTER 6
A PRACTICAL PLAN FOR CHANGE

2 Corinthians 7:10 states: **"For godly grief produces a repentance that leads to salvation without regret, whereas worldly grief produces death."** Godly grief produces a repentance that saves the addict without any regret! No regret. If your addicted loved one regrets the changes that are required, then you may not have an addict who has experienced "godly grief" producing repentance. Your addicted loved one may have only experienced "worldly grief" that only produces death. If the addict is truly sorry because he or she has offended God, then you will see a repentant heart with godly attitudes desiring change, because those changes will lead to pleasing God.

The addict must be willing to be discipled. He or she must be teachable, intentional, and submissive to the discipler. As you know, this is a process, so you must be lovingly confrontational. You must "speak the truth in love"[27] to the addict. Be firm but fair. Be forewarned, however, that you will have to confront the addict's thinking quite often. The old adage about addicts says this: "How do you know when an addict is lying? When he opens his mouth!" This saying will seem true at first but it will get better as the Holy Spirit works.

Change does not occur in the theoretical realm or in generalities. Change happens when it is tangible and measurable. A plan for change must be practical, measurable, and specific. You will need to sit down with the willing addict to adopt a practical plan for repentance. Again, if the addict is willing, he or she will want to help you devise a plan for change. You will not agree about every part of the plan, but you are the leader and the addict is the disciple. Therefore, the addict must submit to your loving leadership.

Sit down together and make a structured plan. Use Appendix E to help you. Be as specific as you possibly can. For example, rather than say, "Be home by dark," put down a specific time: "Be home by 9 pm." Specificity leaves no wiggle room and keeps responsibilities clearly defined.

---

[27] Ephesians 4:15.

Divine Intervention

Be as comprehensive as you want. List daily activities and responsibilities required for the addict. List the expectations in spending time together: "Meet twice weekly (on Wed. and Sunday) to talk for at least 45 minutes to update me, share struggles, pray, and read the Bible together." Do not leave anything off the plan that you think is important. You can even plan out each day in blocks of time specifying the activity to be completed during that time. The addict must establish habit patterns that are positive, effective, and Christ-honoring.

Make an "approved friends list" with whom the addict may communicate. Specify appropriate times for phone calling, bed time, wake time, music, and other privileges. You are only limited by your own conscience, imagination, and the Word of God when devising a specific plan for repentance and practical change.

In the plan for change, I recommend daily Bible study and prayer for the addicted loved one. In reality, once per day of Bible study and prayer is not enough for the addict who must turn their addiction to temporary pleasures into an "addiction for studying God's Word." It is an "addiction to Jesus" so to speak. At least twice per week, you and your addicted loved one should get together for one hour for prayer, fellowship, and Bible study.

Rather than daily self-help group meetings, I recommend daily small group Bible studies or worship services. At very large churches, there are often daily Bible studies that are offered to the congregation and to the community at large. For every day that your addicted loved one does not go to a church worship service, you should find a small group Bible study to attend. If you must, start one in your home for the addict and selected Christian persons.

When starting a small group in your home, invite three to five persons of the same sex as your addicted loved one to participate. Provide food and drinks and lead a Bible study specifically targeted to addiction. If you are unsure of what the Bible says about addiction, go through The Heart of Addiction chapter by chapter. Then go through The Heart of Addiction Workbook chapter by chapter once a good rapport has been established within the group members. The reason you do the workbook second is so that persons in the small group will feel more comfortable sharing their answers from the workbook. Allow the group to continue indefinitely. I know of small groups that have been gathering for breakfast every Saturday for nearly forty years!

Additionally, I strongly recommend biblical counseling at least once per week. In the beginning, two to three meetings each week may be needed, depending upon the type of addiction. Good biblical counseling requires homework assignments of the addict as well, so that the addict learns to turn to God's Word and the Holy Spirit rather than to the counselor. Give the addicted loved one a small to medium sized book to read a chapter each day. Then require a report on it to be given to you. Any "free time" can be spent reading good teaching about the Word of God.

Daily journaling is an excellent way to write out thoughts, prayers to the Lord, goals, accomplishments, and what is being learned. Encourage the addict to share the journal occasionally with a trusted Christian friend. Journals are great to reflect upon after a few months of non-addicted living. They can be extremely encouraging to the transforming addict. They can be humbling, too, in that the addict may be reminded about his or her childishness and selfishness while in the early stages of transformation. Humility is not a bad thing!

You cannot be everything to the addict; therefore, get a trusted Christian friend from the church to meet with your addicted loved one once weekly if possible. A more mature believer in Christ is best and a church deacon, elder, or pastor is an excellent choice. Try to get as many healthy people resources and relationships involved in the addict's life as possible.

I recommend at least a three month commitment (six months is even better) for the plan for change. You and the addict can re-evaluate it after an agreed upon time, but do not allow your addicted loved one to stop the good habits. The addict is building a new standard of living with habits intended to last an entire lifetime; therefore, much of the plan will continue for the rest of the addict's life with some minor changes here and there. Tweaking is allowed and encouraged so that the plan for repentance will be a success.

The Three Steps for Change

On the plan for repentance, have the addict list "put-off" thoughts, words, and behaviors in a column on the left side of the paper. Then ask them to list "put-on" thoughts, words, and behaviors on the right side of the paper next to the corresponding "put-off." For each "put-off and put-on," try to have a biblical verse to support the new, replacement behavior. Following is a guide for helping you and your addicted loved one to develop your own list of "put-off's and put-on's":

The Put-off and Put-on Dynamic

For the repentant addict, the first step in a practical plan of change is obvious: put-off any addictive behaviors. In other words, the addict must stop any and all addictive activities and addiction-related behaviors, such as talking on a cell phone, driving a car, using credit cards, keeping cash in the wallet, and contacting certain people associated with the addiction, including family and friends, if necessary. Major life changes may have to occur in the "putting off" plan. To the extent that a change in employment is necessary, changing jobs due to the bad influence of co-workers might be required. There are too many behaviors to list here; therefore, sit down with your addicted loved one and ask every question you can conjure up to find out what may "trigger" a response leading to a physiological craving.

To get started ask, "Now, tell me, what (who, where, when, why, and how) do you need to stop doing (put-off) right now because it may trigger a "relapse"?[28] If the addict is repentant, they will be honest with you. There may be temptations that they will face that were not brought to mind initially, but that is normal. When those trials and temptations surface, the addict must be encouraged to share them with you in order to develop a plan for avoiding them in the future. They cannot entirely avoid all temptations. It is impossible. However, at this stage in the process, they must exercise wisdom in avoiding those temptations that are known to be stumbling blocks. James 1:14-15 states: **"But each person is tempted when he is lured and enticed by his own desire. [15] Then desire when it has conceived gives birth to sin, and sin when it is fully grown brings forth death."**

---

[28] Appendix C in The Heart of Addiction has a sample "put-off" and "put-on" list for the addict to use. Since this book is written to you (the loved one of an addict), I recommend you get The Heart of Addiction which is written to the addict specifically.

If the addict never stops giving in to the temptation to partake in the addictive behaviors, he or she will not overcome the addiction completely. They cannot dabble in addictive behavior because each time the desire is fulfilled it will create a physiological response. The addict's body must not experience the addictive pleasure for an extended period of time and likely for the remainder of his or her lifetime. Jesus called this "radical amputation" in Matthew 5:29-30: **"If your right eye causes you to sin, tear it out and throw it away. For it is better that you lose one of your members than that your whole body be thrown into hell. [30] And if your right hand causes you to sin, cut it off and throw it away. For it is better that you lose one of your members than that your whole body go into hell."** It is essential that the addict tear out, throw away, cut off, and put-off any fulfillment of the addictive pleasure so that the physiological appetite will decrease and become more manageable.[29]

If the addict stops here and only completes the "put-off" step of the process, he or she will eventually return to active addiction. The "put-off" is only half of the process. Relapse is imminent because the addict is focusing upon what cannot be done; this leads to anger, bitterness, frustration, and aggravation. This is where the wisdom of God becomes evident because God wants the addict to enjoy life and to focus upon what he or she *can* do: the put-on behaviors. When Adam was in the garden in Genesis 2:16-17: **"And the LORD God commanded the man, saying, 'You may surely eat of every tree of the garden,[17] but of the tree of the knowledge of good and evil you shall not eat, for in the day that you eat of it you shall surely die.'"** Every single tree except for one could be eaten from! There was only one tree that was restricted, and its "forbidden fruit" as it is called became the focus for Adam and Eve during their temptation by Satan.

For this reason, the addict must focus upon what he or she can do rather than what they cannot do. God calls it a "put-on." The addict must be reminded by you – and learn to recall for himself – the "put-on" behaviors that are much more enjoyable than the temporary, pleasurable, yet destructive, behavior of the addiction. A man who is trying to stop his addiction to gambling must see that

---

[29] Regardless of the type of addiction, the addict must see a medical doctor for a physical examination and blood work because of the devastation and destructiveness of the addictive lifestyle.

now he can "put-on" spending time with his family, friends, reading, studying, and helping others. Giving money away will be far more satisfying than wasting it on games of chance. These "put-on" attitudes may not seem that significant at first, but they will result in deeper satisfaction through meaningful relationships with others in the long term. When you first sit down at your meeting with the addict to implement the "plan for change," it is *of utmost importance* that you emphasize the positives and "put-on" behaviors more than you emphasize the "put-off" behaviors.

After several weeks, most repentant addicts who have not been involved in their addiction will have the "fog clear" from their thinking and admit that the "put-on" behaviors are more fun than their addictive behaviors. These same addicts will say that the guilt is now gone and it "feels so good" to be "guilt-free." Now, you can begin to address the addict's thinking processes and do the "put-off/ put-on" dynamic all over again to address the mind and its thoughts. Addictive behaviors must stop prior to effectively changing the thinking because addiction is a "physiological" battle at first.

Until the body's appetite for the pleasure is brought into submission, the addict will not be able to concentrate effectively because his own body will be working against him. This is not an excuse, nor should it be an opportunity, for the addict to return to the addiction because the physiological component of the addiction must be stopped eventually. There really is no good time to stop gratifying the addictive desire, and it will be very difficult depending upon the type of addiction and how often it has been fulfilled by the addict.

Regardless of the type of addiction, the addict must see a medical doctor for a physical examination, tests, and blood work because of the devastation and destructiveness of the addictive lifestyle. Even gamblers, video gamers, and excessive shoppers ought to be under the care of a medical doctor; however, the addict should attempt to overcome the addictive behaviors without the use of any medications if at all possible, in order to deal with the real heart issues causing the addiction.

Now that the addict has "put-off" and "put-on" replacement behaviors, the mind must be renewed. In actuality, the renewing of the mind strengthens the "put-on" step of the process as it is listed second in Ephesians 4:22-24: **"to put off your old self, which belongs to your former manner of life and is corrupt through deceitful desires, ²³ and to be renewed in the spirit of your minds, ²⁴ and to put on the new self, created after the likeness of God in true righteousness and holiness."** The addict must have a mind renewal by the Holy Spirit and God's Word or else they will either switch addictions or relapse. More is mentioned about "speaking the truth in love" and lovingly "confronting" the addict's thinking later in this book.

In my first book, <u>The Heart of Addiction*</u>, I go into more depth about the three steps for change from Ephesians 4:22-24: **"to put off your old self, which belongs to your former manner of life and is corrupt through deceitful desires, ²³ and to be renewed in the spirit of your minds, ²⁴ and to put on the new self, created after the likeness of God in true righteousness and holiness."** Those steps are directly derived from these verses: 1) putting-off ungodly, destructive thoughts, words, and behaviors; 2) renewing the spirit of the mind with biblical truths understood by the illumination of the Holy Spirit; and 3) putting-on righteous, Christ-like thoughts, words, and behaviors. You and the addict must begin putting-off, renewing your thinking, and putting-on in order to change in a manner that pleases God.

Power of the Holy Spirit

Christians cannot rely upon self-help, will power, or strength from within oneself alone. Instead, Christians are totally dependent upon the indwelling power of the Holy Spirit to successfully implement this plan for change. A person must be "born again" of the Holy Spirit. Jesus put it this way in John 3:5-8: **"Jesus answered, 'Truly, truly, I say to you, unless one is born of water and the Spirit, he cannot enter the kingdom of God. ⁶ That which is born of the flesh is flesh, and that which is born of the Spirit is spirit. ⁷ Do not marvel that I said to you, "You must be born again." ⁸ The wind blows where it wishes, and you hear its sound, but you do not know where it comes from or where it goes. So it is with everyone who is born of the Spirit.'"**

There is no way around it. You must be "born again" and you cannot save yourself. Only the Lord can save you from your sins and

* Available through amazon.com

fill you with the Holy Spirit. I do not have a secret formula, magic potion, or special words to say to invoke the Holy Spirit because He is like the "wind" that "blows where it wishes, and you hear its sound, but you do not know where it comes from or where it goes." You are totally dependent upon God the Father to save you and your addicted loved one from your sins and to fill you with the Holy Spirit.

The good news is that true Christians are given the Holy Spirit once they are saved. The Bible teaches that the Holy Spirit indwells you, or lives inside of you according to John 14:17: "even the Spirit of truth, whom the world cannot receive, because it neither sees him nor knows him. You know him, for he dwells with you and will be in you." What a great promise from Jesus' lips: that the Holy Spirit of truth will be in you. He will dwell inside of you!

How the Holy Spirit Works

John 14:26 states: "But the Helper, the Holy Spirit, whom the Father will send in my name, he will teach you all things and bring to your remembrance all that I have said to you." In this verse, you learn two things about the Holy Spirit's role in the Christian's life. First, the Holy Spirit will teach you all things. The Holy Spirit will teach you so that you will be able to understand God's Word. Without the Holy Spirit, the Bible will sound like foolishness to you.

Second, the Holy Spirit will bring to your remembrance all that Jesus has "said to you." Since the entire Bible has one theme, this remembrance of Christ Jesus' Words is not limited to the Gospels. Jesus is the Word that was made flesh[30] and the entire Bible is centered upon God's revelation of Jesus to us. In other words, the Bible is God's character revealed to us by the very Words of God Himself. The Holy Spirit will bring those words to your remembrance.

How do you remember them if you have never read, heard, or been taught them? You cannot remember something that is not in your memory. For this reason, you must read, study, memorize, and meditate upon God's Word. The Bible is so crucial for unleashing the power of God in your life and there is no substitute for God's Word. You cannot take a short cut. You must read it for yourself, or you are limiting the power of the Holy Spirit in your life. The addict must read it, too.

[30] John 1:14.

God's power is manifested in the person who understands His Word by God's illumination and has it readily available in memory. Thinking is so important that the Lord wants you to read, study, memorize, and meditate upon His Word all day so that you can have victorious thoughts, emotions, and actions. When your thinking becomes like God's thinking, look out! You will grow and help your loved ones to grow.

Philippians 2:12-13 states: **"work out your own salvation with fear and trembling, [13] for it is God who works in you, both to will and to work for his good pleasure."** When you do your part – the Lord holds you responsible for praying, studying, reading, memorizing, and meditating upon the Bible – then the Holy Spirit has something to bring to your remembrance. Your memory banks must be filled with His Word. You must think, talk, and act like God who displayed His character in the Person of Jesus the Christ.

There is no such thing as will power from within oneself. God creates the willingness in you to work for His purposes for your life.[31] It brings Him good pleasure to do so. He wants you to accomplish His purposes for your life and He will help you to bring that about; however, you must diligently do your part in terms of filling your memory banks with His Word. Listen to preaching and teaching whenever you can. Read and study it for yourself. Think about His Word throughout your day. Memorize it when you are bored and have nothing to do.

To the woman at the well, Jesus said in John 4:23-24: **"But the hour is coming, and is now here, when the true worshipers will worship the Father in spirit and truth, for the Father is seeking such people to worship him. God is spirit, and those who worship him must worship in spirit and truth."** You must be a true worshipper of God and worship Him in the Holy Spirit and in the truth of His Word. You do not worship in your own strength or by your own will power.

Obedience is what the Lord requires from you and your addicted loved one. You both must walk in obedience to Him. You walk in obedience by enforcing the consequences for the "plan for change." Your addicted loved one walks in obedience by fulfilling the commitment to abide by the "plan for change." The good news is that

---

[31] Philippians 2:13.

Divine Intervention

God gives you the indwelling power of the Holy Spirit to create in you a willingness to obey and the power to carry it out.

God gave you resources such as His Word and the indwelling Spirit to enable you to obey Him. You and your addicted loved one cannot just talk about obeying God. You must do the right things that please God according to His revealed Word of truth. It may be very difficult for you to enforce the consequences of violations of the "plan for action." You must encourage, teach, and disciple as much as you rebuke your addicted loved one. Remember that "the kingdom of God does not consist in talk but in power" according to I Corinthians 4:20. Stop talking and start walking in power today[32] and see what the Lord will do to grant repentance and lasting change for your addicted loved one.

---

[32] By "walking," I mean acting, actions, deeds, and doing.

SECTION 3
WHAT THE LORD
WANTS YOU TO LEARN

Divine Intervention

CHAPTER 7
SPEAKING THE TRUTH IN LOVE

Nearly every word that comes out of the mouth of your addicted loved one will be wrong at first. You will need to be confrontational for the addict's benefit to change their thinking. That may sound extreme, but it is true. Addicts have believed the lies of Satan and this world for so long that they are often unaware of the lies in relation to the truth of Christ Jesus. You will have to set your mind to "confront" their addictive, flawed, man-centered, self-centered thoughts, words, and actions, especially in the beginning of the transformation process.

By confrontation, I mean that you must "speak the truth in love" from Ephesians 4:15. In addition, you must exhibit a heart attitude of gentleness, meekness, and humility according to Galatians 6:1: **"Brothers, if anyone is caught in any transgression, you who are spiritual should restore him in a spirit of gentleness. Keep watch on yourself, lest you too be tempted."** When the word "confront" is used, some people think it is harsh, but that is not what is meant here.

Instead, by "confronting," you are admonishing and warning the addict about the lie that is being promoted. If not confronted with the truth in love, that lie may lead the addict back into active addiction. If you love them, then you must warn, admonish, and discipline the addict for this very reason. A truthful confrontation can be gently stated and received effectively when it is "wrapped in love." Practice refraining from getting emotionally charged up in anger or hurt when the addict states a lie to you. Speak the truth in love with your emotions under control and you will see greater effectiveness long-term. Remember that your goal must be to please God in all you think, say, and do. A goal of helping your addicted loved one is a good goal, but it is secondary to the goal of obeying and pleasing the Lord.

Practical Help for Identifying Lies

Do you remember the "put-off" and "put-on" teaching from an earlier chapter? If so, then that is exactly what is needed when you confront the addict by speaking the truth in love. Before you can speak the truth, you must learn those truths that apply to the situation from God's Word. Spend time studying the Bible to find topics of interest that matter to your situation. When you study the Bible with purpose, it is much more rewarding and beneficial to you. To help your addicted loved one, you need to have your weapon of the "sword of the Spirit" ready to go at all times. That weapon is God's Word saturating your mind and its thinking.

There is no shortcut or download in your brain that you can do to put God's Word in your mind. You must read, study, meditate, and memorize His Word daily. Think of it as a daily nutritional plan. Feast upon His Word three times a day as you would at breakfast, lunch, and dinner. Eat a balanced daily diet of fruits, vegetables, and meats consisting of a little Old Testament, New Testament, psalms, and proverbs. Listen to good sermons and read good books that teach the deep truths of the Word of God. You are not limited to one devotional per day! You are limited to your own willingness to read the Bible often.

Even if you are not a biblical scholar, you can still identify the lies of Satan and this world when the addict speaks those to you. Listen for lies like "I'll never overcome this addiction" and replace it with the truth that "I can do all things through Christ who strengthens me."[33] Other lies will be more subtle like "this is my entire fault and I do not deserve any better so I'm just going to go fulfill my addictive desires." While it is true that the consequences of addiction are the addict's fault, and they do not deserve anything better, Christians are called to obey God regardless of their circumstances, so giving into the addictive desire is a sin. Romans 12:21 commands the addict: **"Do not be overcome by evil, but overcome evil with good."** The addict cannot be overcome by all of the evil and hardships in their life, even if they were the cause of it. The addict must overcome evil by doing what is right in the eyes of the Lord which is by doing what is good.

Do not allow lies to be spoken without rebuking them and casting them down. God is not a liar so He wants us to be truth-tellers, and the addict who is speaking lies is not acting like Christ. It is sin and often leads to a defeated attitude that will eventually turn them back to an addiction for relief. While outright lies are very dangerous, half-truths are even more dangerous because they are so hard to discern. A half-truth will have a lie mixed with the truth so it will sound true at first.

---

[33] Philippians 4:13. This verse refers to being content which is a state of mind the addict desperately needs.

Addicts lie so much that many of the lies are half-truth deceptions. If the half-truth is not confronted, corrected, and replaced with the whole truth, the addict will continue to believe the lie.

Matthew 12:34b states: **"For out of the abundance of the heart the mouth speaks."** What this verse teaches is that the lie is already a belief of the addict, and it reveals the addict's heart. Therefore, you must confront this inner, heart attitude with the truth of God. You do not confront it with your own beliefs, but you confront it with God's Word. After you confront it, then you replace the lie with the biblical truth which is often the exact opposite idea of the lie. It is a simple concept but a difficult one to implement.

You must be intentional with the addict. You cannot be unassuming and allow lies to be spoken. Be intentional when you listen and dispel those lies of Satan, who is the author of lies. Your addicted loved one needs the truth of God's Word and is erring because of the addict's lack of power and understanding of God's Word. The power for overcoming the addictive problem cannot be separated from the Word of God! Jesus confronted the lies of the Sadducees regarding the resurrection in Matthew 22:29: **"But Jesus answered them, 'You are wrong, because you know neither the Scriptures nor the power of God.'"**

Do not let your view of Christianity be weak in that you fail to confront lies and reprove the evil works of the devil. The world views Christianity as weak because many times we fail to take a strong stance on what is right. Jesus rebuked Satan with the Word of God[34] and confronted those who believed lies in order to bring them to knowledge of the truth. Jesus knew that reading, studying, memorizing, meditating, and abiding in the truth brings true power and freedom in Christ. John 8:31 states: **"So Jesus said to the Jews who had believed in him, 'If you abide in my word, you are truly my disciples, [32] and you will know the truth, and the truth will set you free.'"**

The Victim Mentality

Probably the most important mindset of lies you will have to confront is the "victim mentality." "Woe is me" says the addict mired in self-pity with the victim mentality. If I had a nickel for every time an addict has made a self-proclaimed "victim mentality" statement to

[34] Matthew 4.

me, I would be a very wealthy counselor. Addicts love thinking they are victims because it takes the responsibility off of their shoulders.

By "victim mentality," I am referring to the "it's not my fault" idea that an addict has. "I have a disease of addiction" is the next thing you will hear from an addict's mouth. But addicts do not stop there; they play the self-pity card as a form of emotional manipulation.

Think about it. If someone is a true victim, you will not confront them with the truth. For example, someone who is truly a victim is a person who has lost their home due to flooding. Are you going to confront this homeless person to deal with any of the homeless victim's sin? No, you are going to be supportive, caring, and encouraging. You will speak the truth in love but you will not need to confront the homeless person because he or she is truly a victim of circumstances beyond their control.

The addict wants this same "free pass" to avoid confrontation. But is it the addict's fault that he or she has become addicted? Yes. In the beginning, the addict made the choice to experience the addictive pleasure. Somewhere down the road that pleasure became physically addictive to their mind and body, causing them to believe they cannot live without the pleasure. The addict believes that he or she cannot stop wanting the pleasure and becomes enslaved to the sin.

The fact remains, however, that the initial choice was the addict's act of the will. They are responsible for the first decision. It was not a mistake. It probably was a sinful choice to please self rather than to please God. While it may have been a misinformed choice, it was still their willful decision. By misinformed, I mean that the addict was likely not aware of the horrible consequences of that choice and how it would lead to such devastation in their life. Nonetheless, no one knows how the decisions we make today will affect tomorrow's quality of life.

Choices for addiction cause the consequences of separation from God and loved ones. Addicts lose the very relationships they need because of the selfishness that an addiction produces. Addicts lose finances, cars, homes, and other material possessions as well. No matter what the devastation of addiction produces, do not allow the addict to think he or she is a victim of circumstances. I am not a fan of the "theory of addiction as a disease", since it is only a man-made theory. The Bible calls drunkenness and idolatry a sin, not an addiction. God holds us all accountable for our sins, and we know that Christians are forgiven of their sins through the blood sacrifice, death, burial, and resurrection of Jesus Christ when there is repentance.

The problem with addiction as a "disease" is that Jesus did not die on the cross for a disease. Jesus died on the cross for our sins. When you call an addiction sin, there is an answer for the sin problem: forgiveness. When you call addiction a "disease," there is no answer, because the addict is not to blame for his or her "disease." Do you know who is to blame for this supposed "disease" of addiction? God. The "disease" concept ultimately blames God because He created the addict with a "diseased" body and a propensity for addictive thinking and behavior.

How sad! The Bible tells us that the first sinners were Adam and Eve and that we are now born with a sin nature. **We see in Genesis 3:12 that Adam blamed God for his eating the fruit in the Garden of Eden: "The man said, "The woman whom you gave to be with me, she gave me fruit of the tree, and I ate."** Did you catch it? Adam said to God, "the woman who YOU gave to be with me" caused my sin, so Adam was not blaming just Eve. Adam blamed God as well.

When we take responsibility for our sins, confess our sins, and forsake our sins, then there is mercy, grace, and forgiveness. Proverbs 28:13 states: **"Whoever conceals his transgressions will not prosper, but he who confesses and forsakes them will obtain mercy."** All of those good things (mercy, grace, and forgiveness) start with taking responsibility. For this reason, it is vitally important that an addict must not be allowed to think he or she is a victim.

Conclusion

Speaking the truth in love to an addict is not easy. You may not be very good at it. It is probably something you have avoided in the past, so you wouldn't have to deal with the bad attitude of the addict, or to avoid a disagreement of some sort. Now, you also must repent from your old ways of thinking and acting by replacing them with new, biblical ways of thinking and acting. You are in a transformation process of growing in the grace and knowledge of the Lord Jesus Christ, too.

Divine Intervention

CHAPTER 8
"CONTROLLING" THE ADDICT

One of the common struggles for family members and close friends of an addict is the matter of control. Even the repentant addict often hates structure, rules, discipline, and submitting to an authority, but these are the very mechanisms that they must embrace to change. You will be viewed by the addict as "controlling." Technically, you <u>are</u> in "control" of many things in the addict's life. Hopefully, the addict can live with someone else who is not a family member, but who is a committed, mature Christian, so that you will not be seen as "controlling."

The perception of you as being "controlling" is not fixable on your part. All you can do is remind the addict of the choices he or she made that put them into this position of having to submit to you and others. Yes, you are in control of many aspects of the addict's life because they have proven to be irresponsible. You are trying to help the addict by loving them and taking charge of the God-given responsibilities they allowed to be neglected or damaged.

If that is controlling, then so be it. You are not running for an election in which you desire the addict's vote; therefore, you do not need to please them. Please the Lord first and the addict will be pleased in the long-term (not the short-term usually!). You are not in control of the addict's perceptions.

God Is In Control

Whether you realize it or not, God is in control because He is sovereign over all things. The addict must be reminded that the Lord has placed you in a position of some control over them for their benefit. God is spirit so the addict cannot technically submit to an invisible, intangible spirit. The way that the addict submits to God is by submitting to you and other authorities that the Lord has ordained. The visible authorities, (you, and others), that the addict must submit to allow the addict to indirectly and ultimately submit to the Lord.

Now, let's put the addict's perceptions aside and pretend that you really are being sinfully "controlling". This type of problem is as common for the family members of an addict as it is for the leaders of God's church who are charged with shepherding God's flock. 1 Peter 5:1-3 states: **"So I exhort the elders among you, as a fellow elder and a witness of the sufferings of Christ, as well as a partaker in the glory that is going to be revealed:** [2] **shepherd the flock of God that is among you, exercising oversight, not under compulsion, but willingly, as God would have you; not for shameful gain, but eagerly;- not domineering over those in your charge, but being examples to the flock."**

Like these elders, you can cross the line of biblical authority when you impose "unscriptural and human inventions upon them instead of necessary duty."[35] In Matthew 20:25-28, Jesus had to deal with this same type of prideful mentality of James and John who desired to rule over others: "But Jesus called them to him and said, **"You know that the rulers of the Gentiles lord it over them, and their great ones exercise authority over them.** [26] **It shall not be so among you. But whoever would be great among you must be your servant,** [27] **and whoever would be first among you must be your slave,** [28] **even as the Son of Man came not to be served but to serve, and to give his life as a ransom for many."**

You are to serve the addict as a "servant leader" rather than a tyrannical dictator. You are not to coerce the addict into doing anything. Instead, you are simply to provide the authoritative structure and schedule under which they are to operate. You are also to be the enforcer of the rules and agreed upon consequences for their poor choices. You must allow the addict the freedom to make choices underneath this framework with knowledge of what the consequences will be if the decision is made to violate the rules.

Certainly, you can offer biblical advice and counsel to the addict about the choice he or she is about to make. However, you are not allowed to use emotional guilt, shame, or manipulation to get them to make the "right" decision. The decision belongs to the addict and sometimes they must fail in order to learn valuable lessons. God's plan may be for the addict to fail and suffer the consequences. You must not attempt to interfere with God's plan. You are not to pretend to be their god.

You are a steward and not the owner of the addict. Even if you are

---

[35] Henry, M. 1996, c1991. *Matthew Henry's Commentary on the Whole Bible: Complete and Unabridged in One Volume* . Hendrickson: Peabody

a parent, you did not create the addict: God did. You are to be a wise steward, or manager, of this power and authority that the Lord has granted you over the addict, but you are to allow the addict to make decisions. It is the only way an addict will learn and it allows the addict to take responsibility.

When you make a decision for the addict, you are taking too much responsibility and rendering the addict powerless. You make them dependent upon you and that is what they resent. You can offer counsel, but when the addict makes the actual decision, he or she will gain responsibility, observe the outcome, and learn a life lesson. Chances are you took on too much responsibility in the past in your relationship with the addict. If so, you were trying to control the addict.

Even if your desire to control the addict was motivated by a good desire for the addict's protection, you were committing sin. You must confess it, ask God's forgiveness, and repent of this sin by understanding where you are responsible, and where the addict is responsible for his or her actions. This may very well be the most difficult challenge facing you, but it can be successfully executed in love and by the leading of the Holy Spirit. Say to yourself what Jesus said to the Father in Luke 22:42: **"Father, if you are willing, remove this cup from me. Nevertheless, not my will, but yours, be done."**

Do not do your will but do the Father's will, which is to cease your efforts to control things that are not your responsibility. Let God be God because He will be God whether you try to be or not. It is utter foolishness to think that you can control the circumstances and decisions of your addicted loved one. You can only control that which the Lord gives you the authority to control. The addict needs to begin to make decisions and to learn from the consequences of those decisions. They will learn the lessons that the Lord wants taught. The addict is in good hands because the addict is in God's Hands.

Divine Intervention

CHAPTER 9
THE "PROGRAM"

Many people today think that addicts must have a "program" to work through and follow or else they will "relapse." I am not a proponent of the "one-size fits all" program mentality for helping addicts. The heart issues of addiction are far too complicated and different among addicts to think that one program is going to resolve most of the issues of the addict. It is a foolish idea but it was perpetuated by treatment and rehabilitation centers. While these places may desire to help addicts in the best way they know how, the truth is that financial constraints and considerations are behind this program mentality.

It is much more cost effective to have "group" counseling than to have "individual" counseling for fifteen men in a treatment center program. Think about it this way: If you owned a treatment center, would you want to counsel fifteen men for one hour apiece totaling fifteen hours or would you want to counsel all fifteen men at the same time for three hours? Which is more cost effective? Which requires less time? Obviously, you can hire fewer counselors when you do "group" counseling, so that is what is done today by most centers.

Does "group" counseling really resolve the issues of the addict effectively? The answer is "no." I am not opposed to some "group" meetings, but the idea of "group" counseling is not always the most effective way to resolve issues.

The transforming, Christian addict needs to be around other Christians. You cannot be the only source of counsel and truth to the addict. One required stipulation for the addict is to begin a relationship with a trusted Christian friend for discipleship purposes. Also, find a biblical counselor in your area who will work with the addict from a scriptural perspective rather than a man-centered one.[36] A monthly meeting with the pastor, assistant pastor, elder, deacon, or Christian leader in the church is helpful, too.

---

[36] I recommend you look at the following website to find a counselor in your area: www.nanc.org.

Get as many people resources as you can involved in the addict's life. You do not need a program to implement in order to begin the transformation process in the addict's mind, heart, and actions. Jesus did not run His disciples through a program. Instead, Jesus lived with His disciples so that they could learn from Him in the real life, teachable moments as well as from His sermons. Jesus established a relationship with His disciples, and that is precisely what the addict needs: healthy, Christian relationships.

The addict who has healthy, Christian relationships will become less self-focused and more focused upon others. This aspect of teaching them to think of others first, and to sacrificially help them cannot be overlooked. The addict can visit nursing homes, orphanages, hospitals, youth detention centers, and the like so that he or she can gain a healthy perspective about how good they really have it compared to those suffering in those institutions.

Remember that the addict lived to fulfill selfish desires for so long that it will be uncomfortable at first to develop meaningful "give and take" relationships. Relationships that are "one-sided" rather than "give and take" often end prematurely because the one person who is only giving and never taking will soon tire of that relationship. The addict can probably list ten relationships that have ended because of their selfish, self-centeredness. Therefore, strongly encourage opportunities for them to work on giving to others either relationally or in a type of service or ministry.

Resources to Use

You may be thinking, "Well, you say no to a program, but what am I supposed to do with my addicted loved one for the next three months?" I am glad you asked that question. There are a lot of great resources you can utilize for your tailor-made "program" which is not really a program at all. It is a relationally-designed, discipleship structure with a practical plan for change. Within that structure, you will want the addict going to daily worship or Bible fellowships, meetings, and studies.

At home, the addict must be reading the Bible and studying it daily. There are many good Bible studies for the addict to do. See

Appendix G for a list of authors with books and workbooks that would be excellent for the addict to read. <u>The Heart of Addiction Workbook</u> and book are solid Bible studies specifically targeting addiction. I recommend setting daily and weekly goals for reading any book. You may say to the addict, "I'd like you to read a chapter per day of this book."

Also, the addict should be completing written work and not just reading the books. If you are not using a workbook, then buy a notebook for them to journal thoughts and feelings as well as writing chapter summaries or the main points of a chapter. Journaling is an excellent tool for addicts as it allows them to be creative and communicative.

The possibilities are endless for developing your own curriculum. You are teaching the addict. You are discipling the addict to become more Christ-like, so Jesus is your model to follow. Do not think for one moment that your approach to addiction, founded upon God's Word, is inferior to the world's programs in treatment and rehabilitation centers. At best, "worldly programs" are teaching humanistic principles that tell the addict that mankind is inherently good and that God is something of your own making!

God does not fit into mankind's program or box. The Lord will meet the needs of your addicted loved one. You must be sensitive to the problems of anger, hurt, bitterness, men-pleasing, loneliness, pride, selfishness, and others so that you can find books and workbooks to assign to the addict's specific issues. However, you have a sovereign God who promises to take care of the Christian addict and will teach an addict who is willing, intentional, submissive, grateful, responsible, faithful, and teachable. Watch and see what the God of the universe accomplishes in the willing heart of your addicted loved one. You will be amazed!

Divine Intervention

CHAPTER 10
HEART ISSUES

Already in this book, you have learned about your personal, heart issues like men-pleasing, learning to speak the truth in love, controlling the addict, and trusting in Christ. The Lord desires for you to grow through these trials in your life while you attempt to deal with an addicted loved one. What does the Lord want you to learn? Let's take a brief look at the possible desires of your heart and the fruit of the Spirit from Galatians 5:22-23 that you will produce by the power of God.

Men-Pleasing

In Galatians 1:10, Paul rebukes the preaching of the Gospel for the pleasing of man: "For am I now seeking the approval of man, or of God? Or am I trying to please man? If I were still trying to please man, I would not be a servant of Christ." Similarly, you are "preaching" the Gospel by how you live and talk with the addict. You may not think of it as this but you are living out the Gospel truths in front of the addict as a servant of Christ. For this reason, you must not strive to please the addict first, but please the Lord.

Ephesians 5:8-12 tells you to discern what is pleasing to God: **"for at one time you were darkness, but now you are light in the Lord. Walk as children of light[9] (for the fruit of light is found in all that is good and right and true), [10] and try to discern what is pleasing to the Lord. [11] Take no part in the unfruitful works of darkness, but instead expose them. [12] For it is shameful even to speak of the things that they do in secret."**

Like the apostle Paul, you have been entrusted with the Gospel message of truth in terms of how you minister, love, and serve the addict. 1 Thessalonians 2:4: **"but just as we have been approved by God to be entrusted with the gospel, so we speak, not to please man, but to please God who tests our hearts."** Like Paul in this verse, you are to please God and not man because the Lord is testing your heart and conforming it into the likeness and image of Christ Jesus.

The antidote for men-pleasing is speaking the truth in love. You may err one of two ways: 1) you may be more on the truth side of this equation minus the love or 2) you may err on the love side of this equation minus the truth. Either extreme is dangerous. Truth-tellers without love are throwing hand grenades of truth at the addict. They explode on the addict and hurt because there are devoid of love. Likewise, "love-tellers" without truth are encouraging the addict but wrongly so. The addict is encouraged to keep doing the same behaviors because he or she is not receiving any corrective truths to promote repentance and change.

Ephesians 4:15-16 states: **"Rather, speaking the truth in love, we are to grow up in every way into him who is the head, into Christ, [16] from whom the whole body, joined and held together by every joint with which it is equipped, when each part is working properly, makes the body grow so that it builds itself up in love."** Did you know that this verse is saying that you will grow more like Christ when you learn to either add truth to your loving statements or add love to your truthful statements to the addict? The balance is to "speak the truth in love" so that you will become more like Jesus Christ. Both you and your addicted loved one will grow more like Christ, too, when receiving the truth in love.

Like Paul told Timothy, a minister of the Gospel, in 2 Timothy 4:2-5: **"preach the word; be ready in season and out of season; reprove, rebuke, and exhort, with complete patience and teaching. [3] For the time is coming when people will not endure sound teaching, but having itching ears they will accumulate for themselves teachers to suit their own passions, [4] and will turn away from listening to the truth and wander off into myths. [5] As for you, always be sober-minded, endure suffering, do the work of an evangelist, fulfill your ministry."** You can take these words to heart, too, and consider this a charge for you to fulfill your ministry to the addict.

Dealing with Hurt and Rejection

If after all of your work the addict goes back to an addictive lifestyle of selfish and prodigal living, then you may experience deep hurt and rejection. You may feel angry at being used and mistreated. You may be deeply disappointed. If the hurt is not addressed soon, you may become embittered and angry.

First, remember that the addict is responsible before God and is hurting God. He or she has rejected the Lord. You are hurting too, but you must pray for the addict to repent and turn back to the Lord first before reconciling your relationship. That idea of reconciliation with the Lord first and then you is very important or else the addict will not begin to effectively change with lasting results.

Second, your hurt in this relationship is very painful and real. You must pray. Ask God what it is that He desires for you to learn through this trial. Take care that this questioning is righteous and not sinful. Don's ask God with an angry, closed fist, "Why are you doing this to me?" Instead, ask God with a willing, open heart, "Why are you allowing this, Lord? What do You want to teach me?" There is a big difference in these two "why" questions and the Lord desires the latter.

Maybe the Lord is concerned about your desires to please human beings more than to please Him. Everyone struggles with "men-pleasing" to some extent. It is not always a bad thing to please others, but when you desire to please others more than to please God, you end up sinning by taking on too much responsibility. You are responsible for your own thinking, speaking, and behaving. You are not responsible for the addict's responses, choices, decisions, and rejection of you.

Third, turn to a trusted Christian friend for support and help. You don't have to give details of the situation in terms of what the addict is doing, but you must give details about how you are responding to the evil and hurt you are experiencing. Focus upon how you can grow rather than upon what the addict is or is not doing.

When your time, energy, and thoughts are focused upon the evil of the addict, you are giving in to the evil lies and acts of Satan. 1 Peter 5:8: **"Be sober-minded; be watchful. Your adversary the devil prowls around like a roaring lion, seeking someone to devour."** Satan seems to be on the throne of God when he is actually a defeated foe. Satan seems to be stronger than he is because you are only focusing upon Satan and evil rather than upon God and good.

Choose today to focus upon God by studying His Word, praying, worship, and having fellowship with other believers. Remember Peter, who walked on the water until he took his eyes off Jesus? Keep your eyes focused upon Jesus so that you will not sink and be overcome by evil. God is winning the war and the battles. God is on the throne. He is the Creator of all things and is infinitely stronger than Satan who is a created being. God will accomplish His will, His plan, and His purpose for the addict and for you, and it will be for your own good.

Blaming Self (Guilt)

Do you blame yourself for the addict's behavior? Should you? Maybe you did think, say, or act wrongly. If you did, then confess your guilt for those wrongs to Christ and to the addict as soon as possible. Ask for forgiveness from God and from the addict. Then put into place a practical plan to practice thinking, speaking, and acting in a God-pleasing manner.

No matter what you have done, you are not responsible for the addict's response to your evil. You are only responsible for your evil thoughts, words, and deeds, and you must see them as evil and sinful or you will not be motivated to change them. Hating them alone is not enough. You must put a practical plan into place for lasting change to occur. You must practice doing good just as you would practice the piano, guitar, or saxophone in order to improve as a musician.

The addict is responsible for his or her choices and responses to your actions. Other people may have hurt the addict too, but they must learn how to biblically deal with hurt and rejection. All Christians must learn to respond as Christ did to hurt and rejection with a Godly perspective in mind. A Godly perspective is one that sees beyond the personal pain caused and looks to the purpose. "God, why and what are You teaching us?" is a question of someone with a Godly perspective. What good is coming of this situation? Not just the good lessons you are learning, but what about the life lessons that your church leaders, close friends, other family members, and acquaintances of the addict are learning. This situation goes beyond you and your addicted loved one.

If you take the blame for the addict's addiction, then you are making the addict a victim who is no longer responsible. As already covered, this is a very dangerous mentality for the addict to have. Addicts have a "perishing mentality" and do not need another person to blame for their choices for addiction. You are not to blame even though some of the things you may have said and done were wrong. These things may have provoked the addict to anger, guilt, or self-pity, but they are responsible for how they choose to respond to that provocation.

Learning Contentment

A thankful heart is a fruit you will see from an addicted loved one who is ready to repent. It is a fruit you must learn to manifest, too. Philippians 4:11-13 refers to "learning" contentment no matter what your circumstances may be: **"Not that I am speaking of being in need, for I have learned in whatever situation I am to be content. ¹² I know how to be brought low, and I know how to abound. In any and every circumstance, I have learned the secret of facing plenty and hunger, abundance and need. ¹³ I can do all things through him who strengthens me."**

Since contentment is learned, it begins with one's thinking. You may have never conceived of contentment as something to learn, but when you are successful, you unlock a secret of the universe because you will be able to be thankful in all of your circumstances. 1 Thessalonians 5:18 says you are to **"give thanks in all circumstances; for this is the will of God in Christ Jesus for you."** When your thoughts accept your circumstances as being allowed, willed, and determined by a good and powerful God of love, then healing will begin for you.

This verse of Scripture is even more powerful when it is studied within its context. I Thessalonians 5:15-19 states: **"See that no one repays anyone evil for evil, but always seek to do good to one another and to everyone. ¹⁶ Rejoice always, ¹⁷ pray without ceasing, ¹⁸ give thanks in all circumstances; for this is the will of God in Christ Jesus for you. ¹⁹ Do not quench the Spirit."** You already understand that you are not to repay evil for evil, but the idea here is that you are to be content with the circumstances in which the Lord has placed you. Furthermore, you are to "rejoice always," not some of the time, for these circumstances because it is the will of God for you to grow in Christ as you overcome this problem of evil. If you fail to set your mind on thankfulness, gratitude, and contentment, then you will quench the Holy Spirit's power in your life to transform you into the likeness of Christ. This is a profound truth with many implications.

Learning to be content is really learning to trust God. All Christians have moments of doubt and fear; however, these doubts are not to lead you away from trusting God: **"Take care, brothers, lest there be in any of you an evil, unbelieving heart, leading you to fall away from the living God"** (Hebrews 3:12). If you allow your circumstances to cause your heart to doubt the Lord and thereby fall further away from Him, then consider yourself failing in this trial. If, however, you allow your circumstances to cause your heart to turn to God's Word and to trust in Him more deeply than ever before, you may consider yourself succeeding in this trial. When you succeed and overcome by God's grace, He will move you on to the next trial of life designed to build your character into Christ-likeness.

Conclusion

Finally, we will conclude this chapter with some thoughts to challenge you to reflect on your personal reaction to the situation. You are not helpless in this situation, but you are not in control either. There is a difference. You are under the direction and leading of the Holy Spirit, so there are things you can do to help the situation. However, ultimately, the results belong to the Lord's will, plan, and purpose.

If you look for strength from within yourself alone, you will not find it. You must look for strength to come through the indwelling of the Holy Spirit and the Word of God. God is in control whether you "let Him" be or not. It is silliness to say, "I'm going to let God be in control today." God was, is, and will be in control whether you "let Him" or not!

What you should say is, "God, I acknowledge that You are in control today, Lord, no matter what I say or do. Help my prideful, controlling attitude to be changed so that my thinking will be more pleasing to You." Many people today, even Christians, think that God is not sovereign but He most certainly is. You need to fear Him so that you can begin to get wisdom for seeing how you are a part of His plan and not the maker of His plan. Proverbs 1:7 states: **"The fear of the LORD is the beginning of knowledge; fools despise wisdom and instruction."**

Confess a "controlling" attitude as sin and pride against God and then pray daily for Him to demonstrate His sovereignty to you. Read Psalm 139 (and there are many other passages of Scripture) to remind you of God's sovereign power. You have a very big God who is capable of doing all things in a perfectly good manner.

The Bible clearly teaches that God is sovereign and mankind is responsible. Those two teachings are supralogical meaning that, as finite creatures, it is beyond our ability to understand them logically.

The teachings are not illogical but are supralogical (in other words, beyond, or above our capability to logically reconcile the two). Deuteronomy 29:29 states: **"The secret things belong to the LORD our God, but the things that are revealed belong to us and to our children forever, that we may do all the words of this law."** Stop trying to understand the secret things of God because you are not God and will never understand them. Instead, seek to understand the revealed things that God has shown you through His Word ("words of this law"). God loves you and wants to reveal His character and nature to you from His Word of truth.

Your addicted loved one must learn to become more independent from you and more dependent upon the Lord. Does this make sense? You are not the addict's god or source of strength. You may have a desire to "feel needed" but you are only an ambassador of Christ, not Christ Himself. I know you would naturally agree with me, but examine your heart in this matter. Many times, people do not realize that they desire to be needed or to be the savior of the addict more than they desire to point the addict to the real Savior, the Lord Jesus Christ.

Although there may be some other heart issues for you to address, the above problems are most common. I want to encourage you that God's Word is very encouraging and helpful to you. Unfortunately, most people do not read God's Word or study it intentionally to find, in a practical way, answers to their problems. The Bible is not a math book so you won't turn to it to answer your math problems. However, the Bible is a textbook to help you to change your thinking, speaking, and acting into what the Lord desires it to be. The Bible is a textbook for learning more about the wonderful character of God, how to deal with sinful, selfish persons, and how to learn to overcome the sinful, selfish attitudes in your own heart.

Divine Intervention

CHAPTER 11
SPECIFIC RELATIONSHIPS

Being a counselor, I see addicts of all shapes, sizes, and colors. Usually, there is one significant relationship that the addict still has left – either with a loved one, family member, or friend. Everyone else may have given up on them and let them go, except for this one person. Often, this one person has personal, heart issues of their own. In this chapter, I will address for you specific issues in the most common relationships so that you will better know your responsibilities before the Lord.

Husband-Wife

If you are the husband and your wife is addicted, as an example, to prescription drugs, you are called by God to be the spiritual leader of your wife. When she fails to follow your leadership, she is being unsubmissive to the Lord as well as to you. You must speak the truth in love to her by calling her to obedience to Christ. You can say, "Dear wife, I am responsible to you as your spiritual leader and I am deeply concerned about your addiction because it is sin against the Lord and against me. I want you to seek help from the church and biblical counseling. If you will not, then you leave me no other choice but to follow the principles in Matthew 18:15-20. I am doing the first step of Matthew 18 now."

As her leader, you are to protect her as best you can. You must protect her from herself so you must obtain her prescription medications and monitor them closely. You must limit her ability to drive around because her mobility may get her into trouble. At first, these types of limitations may be viewed as being "controlling." However, you must answer to God, and He has called you to love and protect your wife. While there are limitations, protecting your wife is your duty.

Do not be passive and allow your wife to do what she wants, because it will lead to destruction. Get the church leaders and others involved as quickly as possible. Invite an older, more mature Christian female to come over to lovingly confront your wife. If your wife persists in being unrepentant and unwilling to change, you may have to make some difficult decisions such as taking her off the checking account, taking the car away, calling doctors to expose evil works of darkness (lying and deceit) where necessary, and taking credit cards away.

Give her a budget to work with so she can make decisions with the family's money, but do not give her unlimited access to that money. Ask her to get any big purchases pre-approved by you. A budget of $100.00 per week may be all she really needs. She may say she has "needs" when they are really "desires." Be sure to meet her needs of food, shelter, and clothing but you are not required to meet her every desire.

I cannot stress enough that most husbands tend to be passive when married to a wife who is addicted to spending, drugs, alcohol, or whatever. Passive husbands who allow their addicted wives unlimited resources and access to financial means are not helping the situation. A loving husband must restrict his wife because she is demonstrating a lack of self-control. This counseling idea of restricting the wife may be criticized by some but what is a husband to do? Is he to allow his wife to sin? Is he to help her sin by giving her whatever financial support she desires?

If the wife becomes willing to address her addiction biblically, then the situation becomes ideal because she is called by God to honor and obey her husband. Ephesians 5:22-24 states: **"Wives, submit to your own husbands, as to the Lord. For the husband is the head of the wife even as Christ is the head of the church, his body, and is himself its Savior. Now as the church submits to Christ, so also wives should submit in everything to their husbands."** It must be an important command to God if He mentions it twice in three verses!

God makes it easy for the addicted wife who is commanded to "submit in everything" to her husband. The word "everything" here means "everything" except if the husband tells her to sin. If he tells her to sin, the wife cannot obey her husband because she must obey the commands of the Lord first. This issue of not submitting to a sinning husband is usually an infrequent occurrence, so wives will not be able to use this exception to the rule very often.

Marriage is tough enough without having to deal with addictive behavior. However, the husband will learn valuable lessons about leadership through this trial. The husband has to guard against being controlling over the wife while still being protective and restrictive.

This situation will not be easily overcome, but it can end up being very rewarding when repentance comes because of the "natural fit" of the husband leading the wife. In fact, the marriage can be improved as a result of this trial.

Wife-Husband

Now, the marriage situation where the wife has an addicted husband is far more difficult than the opposite scenario. Here is a situation where a church that engages in church discipline according to Matthew 18 is able to lovingly help this wife. The church's involvement is absolutely essential for this wife because she has lost her spiritual leader, protector, and provider.

Not only has her husband stopped leading, protecting, and providing for her, but he has become a danger and a threat to her. How ironic that she must now protect herself from her God-given protector! Trust is completely lost in this scenario. A wife in this situation can really begin to doubt God's goodness, and that can lead to hard-heartedness. For this reason, you can see why the church's intervention is so important to this situation because it can demonstrate God's love and provision to her.

If the husband is unrepentant, the wife must appeal to the church for leadership. What a mess! The husband cannot be trusted with finances so she must take precautions and not enable the husband to commit more sin. She may need to separate the bank accounts so that he is responsible for only his own account. She must find ways to limit her husband's access to the house, car, and other financial resources. Again, the husband may view his wife here as controlling and not submissive; however, the wife must answer to God, and He has called her to respect her husband while protecting herself and any children involved.

Do not be passive and allow your husband to do what he wants because it will lead to destruction. Get the church leaders and others involved as quickly as possible. Find an older, more mature Christian male to come over to lovingly confront your husband. If your husband persists in being unrepentant and unwilling to change, then you may have to face some difficult decisions.

If the husband commits adultery and fails to repent, then the wife must consult with her pastor and church leaders to determine if she has grounds for a divorce. While it is usually better to reconcile than divorce, reconciliation depends upon the repentance of the husband. Hopefully, the situation will not worsen to the point of divorce, but it very well could do so. Here again is why church discipline according to Matthew 18 is so vital for its members. The wife must rely upon the church to give her biblical counsel about all of these matters.

If the husband repents for the sin of addiction, then the wife must learn to forgive, trust, and submit to the husband again. These changes are not easy to make when the wife has been living in an exactly opposite manner for years. The husband must be patient with the wife while still trying to help her by lovingly leading and confronting her sin in order for her to grow in Christ and please God. Bad habits can be replaced slowly by beginning to cultivate good habits in the relationship.

Parent-Child

Another common scenario occurs with parents who have an addicted child. It is heart-breaking for parents to see their child destroyed by an addiction. Nevertheless, the child is responsible for his or her actions regardless of the age. For this reason, the parent must foster a structured environment around the child that promotes decision-making with consequences.

An adult child who is living with parents must abide by the parents' rules. While living in that home, the child must honor the house rules. In addition, the child who desires to overcome the addiction needs an agreed upon contract or structure outlining in detail the expectations and rules to follow. It is important to be specific with the establishment of rules and consequences for violations that occur.

A teenage child living with parents is under the parents' authority. The Bible is clear about a child's duties unto the Lord in Ephesians 6:1-3: **"Children, obey your parents in the Lord, for this is right.** [2] **'Honor your father and mother' (this is the first commandment with a promise),** [3] **'that it may go well with you and that you may live long in the land.'** As long as the parent does not tell the child to sin against the Lord, the child is to obey the parents in everything. An addicted child is also commanded to obey parents as unto the Lord. A contract and structure is to be strictly adhered to by the addicted child because it is for the child's benefit and discipline.

A great benefit to the addicted child is to find a same-sex, older person in the church for the child to spend 4 to 8 hours with on a Saturday once each week. This is a discipleship relationship and can be tremendously effective for the child's spiritual growth. At least one of these relationships is recommended but two relationships like this would be beneficial, too. Any more than two, may be too many.

If a teenage child is unruly, ungovernable, and unwilling to repent, then you have a problem. You have what the Bible describes as a scoffer in your home. You must take every privilege away from the scoffer and simply provide for needs only: food, modest clothing, and shelter. Ask the church to help you. Find service work for the teen to do. Find a person for whom the teen may volunteer to do work.

The idea is to keep the teen busy. A famous general once kept his men busy in the bleak cold winter by commanding the building a fort until it was time to leave. During those few months of building the fort, the men worked hard. When the general told them it was time to go, they asked, "What about this fort? It's not finished yet." The general told them that they were leaving the fort since it was not needed but intended to be something for them to do together to build morale rather than wait around doing nothing! Likewise, do not allow the teen to become idle.

Before sending the teen off to a boarding school, military school, detention center, treatment program, camp, or the like, do all that you can to create limitations, restrictions, and relational discipleship opportunities for them. It will be difficult but you may be surprised to find a willing, mature Christian in your church who has an "empty nest" and would desire to mentor your child along with you doing the parenting.

Too many parents are not parenting. Peers, teachers, youth pastors, and bosses have more influence than parents for most teenagers today. You may have to cut back your hours or take a leave of absence to spend *quantity* time with the child that God gave you to rear. This child is your responsibility and you must do everything you can to teach your child about what is really important in life: serving, loving, obeying, and honoring God. Deuteronomy 6:6-7 tells you it is your responsibility (not the youth pastor's) to teach your child the Word of God: **"And these words that I command you today shall be on your heart. You shall teach them diligently to your children, and shall** talk of them when you sit in your house, and when you walk by the way, and when you lie down, and when you rise."

Do not take this responsibility lightly. You may need to home school your teen so that the negative peer influences and relationships will be broken. As a parent, you have the authority to choose your child's friends if the child has proven unable to be discerning. God holds you responsible to provide protection, but if the child refuses to obey, then you must discipline the sinful disobedience of your child. Sometimes, an addicted child breaks the law and gets arrested. If this happens, then the child should go to juvenile detention or jail and suffer the consequences of their poor choices. Too many parents "rescue" their children from the consequences of sinful decisions. Do not trust your emotions in such situations. Trust the principles found in the Word of God.

Child-Parent

If you are a child with an addicted parent, you face some difficult decisions. If you are a minor, then you must confide in another adult you can trust: family member, friend, or church leader. Since the addicted parent is caught in some type of sin (lying, drinking or drugging excessively, gluttony, or the like), you can speak to the church about help, and you must not be afraid to be totally honest so that they know all the details.

If your addicted parent is putting you in danger by illegal activity, then you may have to call the police. It sounds terrible, doesn't it, to call the police? However, what the addicted parent is doing may be illegal and the police are to enforce the laws of the government for the citizens' protection. You need protection and that is what the police are there to do. Most likely, you will have to move in with a grandparent, uncle, other family member, or trusted Christian friend until your addicted parent overcomes the addiction. You need to be safe so that you can focus upon pleasing God and doing your best in school.

If you are an adult child with an addicted parent, there is very little you can do. Speak the truth in love to them by telling your parent how the addiction is hurting them as a sin issue, and separating them from having a close relationship with the Lord and loved ones. Tell them you are willing to help, but only if they begin to demonstrate repentance today. Otherwise, you will be forced to separate yourself from having any intimate, close fellowship with them. The choice is theirs and not yours. You are responding to the biblical command given in 1 Corinthians 5:11 to those who act as "drunkards" and claim to be "brothers" in Christ: **"But now I am writing to you not to associate with anyone who bears the name of brother if he is guilty of sexual immorality or greed, or is an idolater, reviler, drunkard, or swindler—not even to eat with such a one."** You are not to associate yourself with such an outward hypocrite even if it is your parent.

Sibling-Sibling

You may have a brother or sister in your family who struggles with addiction. As in the previous paragraph, you must also follow the command in 1 Corinthians 5:11 to not associate with them. This verse is referring to a "brother" in Christ who is in the family of God. If your blood-related brother or sister is a professing Christian, then you should call them to obedience to Christ. If your sibling does not profess to be a believer in Christ, then you must share the Gospel with them because until they become a Christian, they will not overcome the heart problems that cause addiction to manifest.

Pastor-Addicted Church Member

In this scenario as in the all of these, the relationship between the addicted person and the non-addicted person is on the brink of ending. Here again, if you are a pastor with an addicted church member, you must speak the truth in love to them by asking the question, "How can you call yourself a Christian with the way you are acting? Do you really think you are acting as someone who loves Jesus and is following Him closely?"

You must follow the biblical principles in Matthew 18:15-20 in order to call this addicted Christian to repentance and obedience to Christ. If the addicted person fails to repent through that process, then 1 Corinthians 5:11-13 tells you plainly: **"But now I am writing to you not to associate with anyone who bears the name of brother if he is guilty of sexual immorality or greed, or is an idolater, reviler, drunkard, or swindler—not even to eat with such a one. [12] For what have I to do with judging outsiders? Is it not those inside the church whom you are to judge? [13] God judges those outside. 'Purge the**

evil person from among you.'" You must not eat or have intimate fellowship with such a person and you need to purge this evil person from among your congregation to protect the rest of the flock.

This is not easy advice to follow. You are commanded to obey the Lord so you cover all of these decisions with prayer and fasting. These decisions to honor God by purging the church of a professing Christian who acts like an unbeliever are difficult but you must do what is right in the eyes of God as did Shadrach, Meshach, and Abednego in Daniel 3:8-30. Like them, you may feel as though you are in a fiery furnace but know that the Lord is with you throughout this situation.

Friend-Friend

The final scenario is one between a friend and an addicted friend. In some ways, a friend can be more effective in speaking the truth in love than a family member. I encourage you to keep this relationship going as long as it depends upon you. The addicted friend will leave and you will not hear from them for long periods of time, but when you have a chance to speak with them, take it. Be truthful at those times and call them to repentance and obedience to Christ.

If you allow the addict to live in your home, establish a pre-determined set of rules, and agree together that if the addict violates three of them, they will be asked to leave immediately. You must not tolerate disobedience or feel sorry for the addict because that is what got them to this point in the beginning! Be upfront with the addict and be firm when it comes time to "cast out the scoffer" who is scoffing at both the Lord and you when involved in an active addiction.

Someone who is acting as an unbeliever is most likely not a believer in the Lord Jesus Christ according to 1 Corinthians 6:9-11: **"Do you not know that the unrighteous will not inherit the kingdom of God? Do not be deceived: neither the sexually immoral, nor idolaters, nor adulterers, nor men who practice homosexuality, [10] nor thieves, nor the greedy, nor drunkards, nor revilers, nor swindlers will inherit the kingdom of God. [11] And such were some of you. But you were washed, you were sanctified, you were justified in the name of the Lord Jesus Christ and by the Spirit of our God."** Your addicted loved one who is acting like a drunkard and idolater is likely not a Christian.

You cannot save your addicted friend but God can. Pray for Him to do so today. Do not let a drunkard think that he or she is going to inherit the kingdom of God because verse 10 above clearly teaches that the addict (idolater and drunkard are the biblical names) will not. You are not saying it; God has spoken this in His Word. The Gospel is what your addicted friend must hear to begin the process of transformation and freedom from addiction.

Divine Intervention

CHAPTER 12
CONCLUSION

Do not lose faith in the power of Christ to change an addict's heart! You cannot control the situation or change the addict's heart but God can. While your only hope is in God alone, there are many things you can do to help the situation.

- You may have to end the relationship for awhile
- You may have to cast the addict out of your home
- You may have to tell the addict that he or she is not acting like a Christian
- You may have to call the addict to repentance and obedience to Christ
- You may have to involve others such as your church leaders in the process
- You may have to pray and fast
- You may have to restrict the addict's access to financial and material resources
- You may have to speak the truth in love by confronting the addict many times
- You may have to make some very difficult decisions.

One thing is sure: you will learn so much when you do things God's way as outlined in the Bible. Throughout God's Word, there were men and women of faith that faced difficulties and challenges. When these people of faith obeyed the Lord, they overcame their trials. Likewise, when they disobeyed God, they suffered the negative consequences. Is the Lord calling you to obey Him today in your relationship with an addicted loved one?

The discipleship of an addict is not an easy task but the addict desperately needs discipline and structure. You are to disciple the addict in the same way the apostle Paul did according to 1 Thessalonians 2:5-8: **"For we never came with words of flattery, as you know, nor with a pretext for greed—God is witness. ⁶ Nor did we seek glory from people, whether from you or from others, though we could have** made demands as apostles of Christ. **⁷ But we were gentle among you, like a nursing mother taking care of her own children. ⁸ So, being affectionately desirous of you, we were ready to share with you not only the gospel of God but also our own selves, because you had become very dear to us."** You want to foster a healthy relationship with the addict to create an atmosphere of speaking the truth in love.

Not only will the addict grow, but you will grow into Christ, too, when you acknowledge the truth in love. **"Rather, speaking the truth in love, we are to grow up in every way into him who is the head, into Christ"** (Ephesians 4:15). You will become less controlling, more accepting of God's sovereignty in your circumstances, and better able to identify the heart issues that the Holy Spirit is transforming in you. By speaking the truth, you stop living a lie with your addicted loved one who is openly rebelling against the Lord. By being loving, you are gently, meekly, and humbly setting limits and enforcing the pre-determined consequences, which encourages your addicted loved one to grow more independent from you and more dependent upon the Lord.

Your addicted loved one's process of transformation – of becoming more Christ-like – requires the truth in love. Learn the truth from His Word of truth, and allow the love of God as shown by the Holy Spirit to work in your heart today. Do not grow weary in doing the right things in God's eyes. 2 Thessalonians 3:13-15: **"As for you, brothers, do not grow weary in doing good. ¹⁴ If anyone does not obey what we say in this letter, take note of that person, and have nothing to do with him, that he may be ashamed. ¹⁵ Do not regard him as an enemy, but warn him as a brother."**

APPENDIX A
ENABLING THOUGHTS, WORDS, AND ACTIONS

Listed below are some of the common "enabling" thoughts, words, and actions that you may be having or have had in the past. Understand that the majority of the items on this list are your sinful attitudes and responses that must be confessed and forsaken (Proverbs 28:13).

Review the list and place a check next to any of these that apply to you. The list may provoke you to think of a few more so be sure to add those at the end of this list. Then, write an opposite, "put-on" thought to replace each "put-off" thought listed below. A few examples are given but you need to 1) earnestly consider your "put-on" thought, 2) put that thought into your own words, and 3) be sure it is supported by Scripture.

In some situations, it is fruitful to give the addict the opportunity to look at this list and help identify your enabling thoughts, words, and actions. This exercise may give you more insight and may cause the addict to recognize the unhealthiness of the relationship the two of you share. Hopefully, this list will lead you, and possibly the addict as well, to true repentance.

What thoughts and actions of mine are enabling my addicted loved one?

Checklist:

After you ask me multiple times, I give in to you and give you what you want, even when I know it is wrong.

Put-on: "Even after you ask multiple times, I will do what is right in the sight of God and refuse to give it to you." (Ephesians 5:11)

I give you multiple warnings, without following through with consequences.

Put-on: "I will give you one warning and then follow through with the appropriate consequence for your choice" (Proverbs 19:19).

I have been more worried about my reputation (with outsiders in the world) than I have been concerned about your heart.

Put-on: "I will not be primarily concerned about men-pleasing. Instead, I will do what is pleasing to God and seek to help you to please Him, too" (Matthew 6:33 and 1 Thessalonians 2:4).

O I have given you no clearly defined expectations in our relationship.

O I have thought too much about how my actions of giving you consequences would make me look.

O I have worried about what might happen if I didn't help you get out of your troubles.

O I worry about how I might feel guilty if you were to die from your addiction.

O I have worried more about your external appearances than your heart attitudes toward God.

O I have made excuses for your failure to achieve high standards of behavior or your commission of immoral acts (i.e. I have had thoughts like, "The reason your grades were poor was because you had to work to support yourself through school," or, "The reason you talked harshly to me or your teachers was because you were so tired and your Dad was mean to you last night.")

O I have shared the above excuses out loud (verbally) with you.

O I have tried to make up for the poor treatment you got as a small child by giving you pleasurable things.

O I allow for too much leeway in my restricting or correcting or calling you to repentance for your actions.

O I have allowed my pity parties to become yours by sharing them with you aloud.

- O I have allowed your pity parties to become mine by indulging in and listening to your complaining.

- O I have allowed and participated in drunken acts of pleasure and _____ with you.

- O I have allowed and/or participated in actions that were dishonoring and disrespectful of your God-given authority figures (i.e. father, mother, teacher, or employer).

- O I have allowed and/or participated in dishonoring and disrespectful answers to you (returning evil for evil and railing for railing).

- O I have allowed and/or participated in physical demonstrations of my anger toward you (i.e. hitting, scratching, biting, pulling hair).

- O I have failed to admit or recognize the presence of hypocrisy in my life as viewed by you or others.

- O I have allowed your accusations of my hypocrisy to prevent us from focusing on your heart toward God (i.e. thoughts like "If I say that about his drinking then he will be more likely to reverse accusations about my problem smoking pot," etc.).

- O I have only said to you, "Do as I say, not as I do," in response to the above.

- O I have failed to rebuke you privately for fear of looking hypocritical in your eyes.

- O I have failed to rebuke you for fear of what others may think of me (not a good husband, wife, mother, son, etc.).

- O I have failed to rebuke you for fear that we would not be able to pay the bills if you lost your job.

- O I have failed to rebuke you for fear that you would not love me.

- O I have failed to rebuke you for fear that you would hate me and never again be a part of my life.

- O I am afraid of what my life would be like without you in it.

- O I have used my guilt or laziness or lack of diligence as an excuse for your sins. (i.e. "I didn't give you a consistent bed time when you were a child, so you were more disobedient, and I let it slide because you were tired." OR "I didn't give you a healthy diet, good clothing, or a home in a nicer neighborhood so you have an excuse for being angry and yelling disrespectfully at me." OR "I didn't have time to teach you how to clean your room so I let it be done by myself or someone else.")

○ I have allowed you to go on in sin by telling myself and you that at least you are not as bad as someone else I know or have heard about. (For more on "comparative morality" phenomenon see chapter 3 in The Heart of Addiction by Mark E. Shaw)

○ I have been a peace lover and not a peace maker. I have avoided conflict rather than trying to resolve it biblically.

○ I have not been asking you questions about your whereabouts because "what I don't know won't hurt me."

○ I ignored your addiction because I was avoiding dealing with it or trying to avoid feeling as though I am responsible for it and thus now I am responsible to help you.

○ I have feared your discomfort or pain.

○ I have not allowed you to feel the pain of God's discipline or any authority's discipline of you.

○ I have allowed my disagreements with your other parent (or _____) to be excuses for your failure to thrive spiritually.

○ I have harbored thoughts and / or feelings of unforgiveness toward you even though you have tried to repent in the past.

○ I demand perfection from you which is wrong and often provokes you to anger.

○ I am critical of you so that you will not criticize me.

○ I am often unloving toward you.

○ I am selfish toward you.

○ I often think I am better than you and that is sinful pride.

○ I am controlling rather than helpful.

○ I try to be your Holy Spirit sometimes.

APPENDIX B

SHARING YOUR FAITH
AND THE GOSPEL

One of the best classes I have ever taken was called "Evangelism Explosion" which was developed by Dr. D. James Kennedy to equip Christians to share the Gospel message, their personal faith, and to promote discipleship and healthy growth in the church. I recommend you read the book or take the class to better equip yourself to share the Gospel and your faith.

Below, I have excerpted a small portion of this book to help you to share your faith with your addicted loved one.[1]

"Three times in the book of Acts, the apostle Paul gave his testimony. Notice in Acts 22 that he set forth the three essential elements of a good testimony:

1. What I was before I received eternal life (vv. 3-5)

2. How I received eternal life (vv. 6-11)

3. What eternal life has meant to me (vv. 12-21)."

As you write your personal testimony, format it into those three categories above. Read Acts 22:3-21 to get a clearer understanding of the elements involved in Paul's testimony so that you can model it. Keep your life history brief and accentuate the Gospel message of grace for sinners. Your personal testimony does not have to be lengthy because you are relying upon the Holy Spirit to do the work through your testimony.

Here are some more helpful hints adapted from Dr. Kennedy's book:[2]

1. Emphasize the positive. This involves sharing how the gospel and salvation have changed your life in a positive way – not necessarily all the trials and hardships since then.

2. Identify with the person to whom you are sharing your faith. Make sure that you are opening up enough of your personal

---

[1] Kennedy, D. James, <u>Evangelism Explosion: Fourth Edition,</u> Wheaton, IL: Tyndale House Publishers, p. 65.

[2] Ibid, p. 68-71.

history prior to salvation that allows that person listening to identify with you and to see themselves in you. Consider the aspects of your life that were similar to the listener's present situation or lifestyle.

3. Do not give answers before you ask questions. This means presenting the problem of sin and uncertainty mounting in your life as a problem that needed solution – without giving the answers to the question of what the real and only solution is. You want the listener to see your sin problem and need for a Savior before you give them the "right" answers. If you simply tell them the "right" answers before you present the problem, then you are just leading them to give you the "right" answers back and addicts are often "people-savvy." In other words, they know how to tell you what you want to hear and it will cause you to be unable to discern whether or not real understanding of the gospel message has taken place.

4. Be specific. People remember specifics, such as, "My life is so free now that I know that God has given me the realization that even if this cancer takes over my whole body, I will be with him in eternity." People do not relate to generalities such as "I now have peace with God."

5. Avoid clichés. "It was such a blessing" is a cliché that may be meaningless to the addict. The addict may wonder, "Well, how do blessings come? What is a blessing? Does it fall from the sky?"

6. Use direct and indirect quotations. Specific quotes make the story more personal and meaningful. For example, "Then I said, 'Lord, I need you; help me to overcome my fear,'" is a quotation from the heart that has relevance and meaning.

7. Avoid giving a travelogue. Details about your travels and where you lived are not important to the real spiritual matters that you want to share.

8. Focus on God's faithfulness. Point to God and His grace in your life that has enabled you to overcome your hardships, not your sinfulness and backsliding details.

9. Use humor constructively. Avoid frivolous attitudes toward the gospel, but it is okay to use humor to lighten the tension appropriately.

10. Speak pictorially. Use images that are memorable to tell the events of your story. Illustrations and metaphors can be helpful, too.

Make your testimony brief, personal, and transparent to the addict for most effectiveness.

Finally, from Dr. Kennedy's book, there are some essential elements to include in your Gospel presentation.[3] For grace, you will want to include that heaven is a "free gift" and "is not earned or deserved." For man, include that "man is a sinner" and "cannot save himself." For God, include that "God is merciful and therefore does not want to punish sin" yet "God is just and therefore must punish sin." For Christ, include who He is: "the infinite God-man." Also, include what He did: "He died on the cross and rose from the dead to pay the penalty for our sins and to purchase a place in heaven for us, which He offers as a gift."

For faith, include "what it is not: mere intellectual assent or mere temporal faith." What this means is that knowledge of God is not faith. Satan has knowledge of God but he does not have saving faith! Faith is not "temporary faith" that produces a good result so one can go back to living in sin. Trusting in God for the things of this world (finances, new job, overcoming an addiction, health, or protection) is not eternal, saving faith in Christ Jesus. Faith is "trusting in Jesus Christ alone for eternal life." Acts 16:31 says: "And they said, "Believe in the Lord Jesus, and you will be saved, you and your household."

At the end of sharing your faith and the Gospel presentation, Dr. Kennedy recommends you ask two questions in this particular order: "Does this make sense to you?" and "Would you like to receive this gift of eternal life?" The Lord uses you and me as instruments in His Hands to lead others to a saving faith in Christ Jesus. Trust Him to lead you.

---

[3] Ibid, p. 31-36.

Divine Intervention

APPENDIX C
SAMPLE "INTERVENTION" LETTER

When you write the "intervention" letter to your addicted loved one, first reaffirm the relationship by assuring him or her of your love and desire to have a healthy relationship with them. For this to occur, you may have to confess your sins in the relationship, commit to working a plan for change yourself, and ask for forgiveness from your addicted loved one. Humility works well in these situations and the Bible commands you to take the "log out of your own eye" before taking the "speck out of your brother's eye" according to Matthew 7:1-5.

Having completed your part of the repentance and forgiveness process, now you can focus upon the addict's sin. As I mentioned in chapter 3, there are four elements to include in your letter. These elements have been based upon 2 Timothy 3:16-17: **"All Scripture is breathed out by God and profitable for teaching, for reproof, for correction, and for training in righteousness, ¹⁷ that the man of God may be competent, equipped for every good work."** You will notice each element in the sample letter that follows:

Dear <u>Addicted Loved One's Name</u>,

I am so glad to get this opportunity to read this letter to you now. I value our relationship. I realize how unhealthy it has been from my standpoint. (If necessary, CONFESS YOUR SIN, PRESENT A BRIEF PLAN FOR YOUR REPENTANCE, and ASK THE ADDICT FOR FORGIVENESS right here.) I have much to learn and a lot to change in myself. However, I believe in the power of Christ to change both of us. I want to help you in any way I can.

(TEACHING) My relationship with you should have been better and will be better. You and I can have a very good relationship that is based on solid, biblical principles for love, understanding, communication, mutual respect, and service to each other. I know it will not be perfect, but I do expect it to be much improved as you and I learn more biblical principles for relating to one another in a healthy manner. I cannot "enable" your addiction any longer.

Divine Intervention

(REPROOF) I admit I have not loved, respected, and communicated with you in a godly manner at times. I have asked God to forgive me and now have asked you to forgive me for these sins. Likewise, you have sinned against me by lying, manipulating, stealing, disrespecting, and being unloving. (You can list a few specific instances here if you like.) Your addiction has created problems not only for you but for many of us who love you. Addiction is a sin problem that requires repentance. You state that you are a Christian and I believe it to be true even though right now I do not see much fruit or evidence of Christ-likeness. In other words, you are not acting as a Christian who is submitted to the power of the Holy Spirit, because you are enslaved to the power of your addiction (Ephesians 5:18). You are destroying the relationships with the very persons who love you the most and you are treating us like objects rather than persons.

(CORRECTION) Because I am concerned for you, I want to tell you that there is hope for change. If you are willing, I will do all I can to help you. You are not an innocent victim to an addiction. You are responsible for your addictive choices and it is sin. The Lord holds you responsible and you can change by His power. The same power that saved you and made you a Christian will change you by making you more Christ-like. You must change or you will lose the relationships with the people who love you most. More importantly, you must change or you will die in these sins. However, it starts today with you. You must be WILLING to change. I know it will be difficult but I know it will be worth it, too.

(DISCIPLINED TRAINING IN RIGHTEOUSNESS) Jesus died on the cross and shed His innocent blood for your sins and mine. Obviously, if Jesus gave up His life for sin, then sin is a big deal to Him. You cannot overcome your addiction fully without acknowledging your actions as sin and taking it to the cross. I know that you can overcome this addiction but it will require repentance and a complete change of mind. I will expect you to attend weekly worship services at church, Bible studies, and fellowship meetings with other believers. I will expect you to pray daily, study your Bible daily, and receive biblical counseling. (Add more expectations here if you like but I recommend not being too specific at this point because you do not want to overwhelm the addict.)

You cannot do this alone. Therefore, I am committed to helping you. The following people are as well: _____ (list as many people as you can here). I spoke to them before this meeting and they agreed to help you as much as they can. We will help you to restructure your life so that you can live in a pleasing manner unto the Lord and begin to serve others with all of your God-given gifts and abilities. You have so much to offer this world and it hurts me to see you squandering your gifts on selfish living in an addiction.

Will you willingly commit to receiving the help you need today? Will you do everything in your power to repent and restructure your life? Will you do these things, not for me or anyone else, but for the Lord because He alone is the One you must seek to please?

Speaking the truth in love,
YOUR NAME

Again, this is just a quick sample. I would not make the letter too long and I would ask for a commitment in word and then in deed (action) immediately. At this point, you will want to get the addict into a new, safe environment (if possible) so as to minimize any temptation to sin. The addict can move into the discipler's home immediately and you can pack some of the addict's essential items ahead of this meeting. You want to move as quickly as possible so do not ask for a commitment in words without immediate actions.

Divine Intervention

APPENDIX D
THE GOSPEL IS "GOOD NEWS"
This gospel presentation has been excerpted with minor revisions and additions from <u>The Heart of Addiction</u>.

If you are reading this section of the book, there is probably some question in your mind as to whether or not you are a Christian. Where you are going to spend eternity should be a big concern to everyone. Unfortunately, many people believe there is no afterlife, but that's not what the Bible teaches. The Bible tells us that life on earth is temporary and there is definitely an afterlife. Those who are born again by the Holy Spirit become Christians and will spend their eternal life with the Heavenly Father. Those who do not become Christians will spend their eternal life in an unspeakably horrible place called Hell. Therefore, everyone will inherit one of these two eternal destinations after life on earth.

Although the Gospel message is good news, you must hear the bad news first. The bad news is that apart from Christ you are helpless and sinful. More bad news is that everyone is a sinner, in spiritual bondage, alienated from God because of sin, and headed for the eternal destination of hell. Knowledge of sin comes by the law of God which is found in His Word of Truth. God, in his justice, punishes sinners. You cannot save yourself in any way from this punishment. God is serious about sin and He will punish sinners who are not saved by grace through their faith in Jesus Christ.

Jesus alone saves you by grace through faith in Him. Eternal life with God is a gracious, free gift from Him. Ephesians 2:8-9 puts it this way: "For by grace you have been saved through faith. And this is not your own doing; it is the gift of God, not a result of works, so that no one may boast." Therefore, you cannot come to God in your own strength, with your good deeds, and ask for eternal life. It is God who draws you to Himself.

Jesus suffered, died, and shed His blood for sinners. The Lord calls sinners like you and me to repent, or turn from sin, and to turn to God. Turning to God is called trusting Him, believing in Him, or having faith in Him to save you. You are given a new heart and a new nature so that you do not have to remain a slave to sin. You are saved in order to joyfully obey and serve the Lord for His own glory and purposes.[4] God's plan and purposes for you may take you in a different direction than you wanted to go, but you can trust His character because He is loving and faithful. God loves His people and no longer sees them as unrepentant sinners, but now sees them as sons who have a relationship with Him.

No one starts out this life in neutral, since everyone is born in sin and then commits more sin during life. No sin is too big for you to repent of and for God to forgive. No one can earn the gift of eternal life nor does anyone deserve it. Eternal life is a free gift such as you would receive at Christmas time: you do not pay for it. Is there any reason why you would not want to pray to receive Jesus Christ as your personal Savior right now? I encourage you to pray right now. A model prayer is the Lord's Prayer in Matthew 6:7-15, but I always recommend that you pray from your heart to God. Do not be concerned about the words you use. In your prayer, confess your sin to God, admit you are a sinner who has lived independently from God, that you have not earned or deserve the free gift of eternal life, and that you desire to have an intimate relationship with God, your Creator, now and forevermore.

When you become a Christian, your new heart and your newly-found love for God causes you to want to do whatever pleases Him because He deserves it and He saved you from the penalty of your sins. Now, you have the Holy Spirit's power living inside you to cause you to **want to** please and obey your Father God, and also to **be able to** please and obey your new Father God.[5]

---

[4] Kruis, John G. Quick Scripture Reference for Counseling, Grand Rapids, MI: Baker Books, p. 6.
[5] Shaw, Mark, The Heart of Addiction, Vestavia Hills, AL: Milestone Books Publishing, p. 195-196 (with minor revisions and additions).

APPENDIX E
SAMPLE "PLAN FOR CHANGE"

One of the primary messages that Jesus preached in the Bible was "Repent!" The addict needs a practical plan for change and repentance. In this appendix, I've outlined a "sample" plan for you to use, tweak, or revamp to your situation. This is not meant to be "legalistic" for the addict, but it is meant to be restrictive so that the addict's temptations to sin are minimized. If the addict willingly agrees to this plan, then it is not "legalism." Therefore, ask the addict for input, but understand that there may be certain requirements that are not negotiable (i.e. church attendance, certain Bible study groups, etc.). If the addict protests, then remind them that in-patient treatment and rehabilitation centers do not ask the addict for input regarding their requirements!

Sunday	Monday	Tuesday	Wednesday	Thursday	Friday	Saturday
7:00 am Prayer	6:00 am Prayer	6:00 am Prayer	6:00 am Prayer	6:00 am Prayer	6:00 am Prayer	7:00 am Prayer
7:30 am Bible	6:30 am Bible	6:30 am Bible	6:30 am Bible	6:30 am Bible	6:30 am Bible	7:30 am Bible
8:00 am B'fast w/Mentor	7:00 am Prep for Work	7:00 am Prep for Work	7:00 am Prep for Work	7:00 am Prep for Work	7:00 am Prep for Work	8:00-noon Serve others*
10:00 am Sun School	7:30 am Leave for Work	7:30 am Leave for Work	7:30 am Leave for Work	7:30 am Leave for Work	7:30 am Leave for Work	
11:00 am Worship	8am - 5pm Work	8am - 5pm Work	8am - 5pm Work	8am - 5pm Work	8am - 5pm Work	Noon - 5:30 free
Noon Lunch**						
1:00 pm Rest & prep for evening***	5:30 pm Be home & prep for evening	5:30 pm Be home & prep for evening	5:30 pm Be home & prep for evening	5:30 pm Be home & prep for evening	5:30 pm Be home & prep for evening	5:30 pm Be home & prep for evening
5:00 Dinner	6:00 Dinner	6:00 Dinner	5:30 Dinner	6:00 Dinner	6:00 Dinner	6:00 Dinner
6:00 pm Worship (church)	6:30 pm Addiction Group (find a group/ start one)	6:30 pm In-home Bible (start group in home)	6:00 pm Worship (church)	6:30 pm Weekly Meeting (w/ mentor)	6:30 pm Fellowship (planned church activity - recreational)****	6:30 pm Fellowship/Fun
9:30 pm Quiet time of Reflection/ Meditation	9:30 pm Quiet time of Reflection/ Meditation	9:30 pm Quiet time of Reflection/ Meditation	9:30 pm Quiet time of Reflection/ Meditation	9:30 pm Quiet time of Reflection/ Meditation	9:30 pm Quiet time of Reflection/ Meditation	9:30 pm Quiet time of Reflection/ Meditation
10:00 pm Lights Out	10:00 pm Lights Out	10:00 pm Lights Out	10:00 pm Lights Out	10:00 pm Lights Out	10:00 pm Lights Out	10:00 pm Lights Out

*Serve others = visit nursing homes, mow someone's yard, wash other's cars, etc. ANYTHING the addict can do for someone other than himself/herself.

**I recommend eating all meals with others when possible. After corporate church worship on Sundays is an opportune time to eat with a pastor, elder, deacon, church member, mentor, trusted Christian friend, etc.

***Prepping for the evening may mean taking a shower, helping with dinner, or getting books ready for study later that evening.

****All the activities on this line are difficult to put in a "sample" because of the variety of your circumstances and situation. I recommend a church worship service on Sunday evening even if your church does not have one. Join a small group on Sunday evening, start one, or find a church to attend. For Monday, Tuesday, Thursday, and Friday, you are limited only by your own investigation into available opportunities for spiritual growth in your community. Again, finding an existing one that is biblically-focused may be a challenge so if you cannot find one, then create your own in your home OR ask your pastor or elders to start one using this book and The Heart of Addiction. I prefer Bible studies to self-help meetings. On Saturdays (and some Fridays), find a church-related recreational event to attend or have the addict attend. Make church a central part of the addict's life even in fun and fellowship.

FINAL NOTES

One final note is that I would require a certain amount of reading, workbook completion, journaling, written work, and the like to be completed each DAY so that the addict knows exactly what is to be turned in each day. For example, write out a schedule for the week or month that reads:

Monday: Read Chapter 1 of The Heart of Addiction

Tuesday: Complete corresponding chapter in The Heart of Addiction Workbook

Wednesday: Read Chapter 2

Thursday: Complete Workbook Chapter 2

Friday: Read Chapter 3

Saturday: Complete Workbook Chapter 3

Sunday: Read Bible only

Be as specific as you would like to be. You can require that the addict leave the day's completed work in a collection tray or box for you to check for accountability purposes. Have the addict log his/her daily reading in a log to be left in that box, too. The possibilities are endless and some of these "tracking" procedures will be developed during the course of action. Be creative and ask the addict for input. Learn and grow together.

Divine Intervention

APPENDIX F
SAMPLE PUT-OFF LIST AND PUT-ON LIST

You can develop your own list with a blank piece of paper, but this appendix is designed to give you ideas and to help you think of things that you may not have considered.[6] You can add anything you want to put-on as long as it is not sinful. Warning: sometimes we make a good thing into an idol which ends up making it a curse rather than a blessing!

THINGS TO PUT-OFF

WHAT:

1. Clothes advertising alcohol and drugs.
2. Cell phones. Too tempting and not needed.
3. Cigarettes. Believe it or not, those who give up smoking improve their ability to stay clean and sober.
4. Coolers used to keep alcoholic drinks cold.
5. Cars. No need to drive for a few months. Ask for rides to work. Humble yourself.
6. Secular books and magazines. You know what to read instead (Hint: Starts with a "B")
7. Television. Too many beer commercials glamorize the drunkard's lifestyle.
8. Internet. Too may temptations to do wrong.

WHERE:

1. Bars and restaurants where you used to "hang out" and drink/drug.
2. Houses of old "using buddies," friends, and "drinking buddies."
3. Convenience stores are too tempting and too easy to pick up a six pack or a cold beer.

---

[6] Appendix is excerpted from <u>The Heart of Addiction</u> by Mark E. Shaw. It is appendix C in that book.

4. Grocery store aisles that have liquor and beer only. You can go to the store; just avoid that particular aisle. Do not even look toward the aisle. Look away when you see it.

5. Friends and relatives' houses that drink, if only for 6 months or so. Avoid temptation.

6. Places, houses, neighborhoods, and streets where you used to buy drugs and alcohol. Drive a different route if necessary.

7. Avoid your place of purchase at all costs and especially if you are alone.

WHO:

1. Some relationships must be put-off permanently while other relationships may only require a temporary put-off.

2. Avoid old drug-using buddies and "friends" permanently.

3. Avoid dealers and shady acquaintances at all costs.

4. Avoid meeting new people alone. Have a friend or relative with you.

5. Some relatives and friends may have to be put-off permanently if they drink/drug.

6. Some relatives who drink may be put-off temporarily until you can confide in them and ask them to help you with your struggles.

7. If single, relationships with the opposite sex often need to be put-off whether you want to or not.

8. Co-workers who encourage drinking and drugging. Do not associate intimately with them while at work and especially after work hours in a social setting.

WHEN:

1. Put-off being alone for long periods of time (an hour may be too long to some while 30 minutes is too long for others)

2. Put-off feelings of hurt and rejection by going to the person who hurt you directly in order to reconcile the relationship.

3. For the first major holidays when you are sober, consider putting-off where you used to spend your holidays so that you can create a new tradition somewhere else, if necessary.

WHY:

1. Perishing mentality must be put-off as it contributes to depression, hopelessness, anger, self-pity, etc.

2. Do not allow yourself to become a pessimist. You must become balanced.

THINGS TO PUT-ON

WHAT:

1. Clothes advertising Jesus Christ, your church, and Bible verses.

2. Meet in person with an elder, deacon, or mature Christian; maybe for coffee or lunch.

3. Chew gum. Put a pocket-sized Bible in the exact place where you carried your cigarettes. They are about the same size so it is a great substitute. Read it when you have a physical craving to smoke.

4. Keep a box of Christian CDs, tapes, evangelistic tracts, and books in your car where you kept your cooler for cold beer!

5. Walk. Exercise is so good for the transforming Christian addict. Check with your physician first!

6. Christian books and magazines. Read the Bible.

7. Read a book instead of watching TV. Write your own book based on Scriptures and your life story.

8. Spend the time you would have spent on the internet or watching TV in a real conversation, face-to-face in fellowship with another Christian believer. Have a real relationship with someone and focus upon helping them in some way.

9. Females: Make a meal for someone else and bring it to them.

10. Males: Offer a friend help/service without expecting anything in return.

11. Drink lots of water to replace your physiological thirst and desires for alcohol. Always be drinking something like water, juice, or healthy, non-alcoholic drinks. Experiment and find tasteful, new healthy drinks that you have not tried before.

Divine Intervention

WHERE:

1. Church, Bible studies, and fellowship meetings with other Christians must be your new "hang out."

2. Invite Christians into your home for fun, fellowship, prayer, or Bible study.

3. Gas up at the pump rather than going into the convenience store.

4. Think about the aisles you can walk down rather than focusing upon the one aisle that you must avoid. Look at the things you can buy and enjoy moderately while at the store.

5. Ask friends and relatives who drink to come over to your house but be clear that they cannot bring alcohol.

6. Plan out a different route to drive home to avoid places, houses, neighborhoods, and streets where you used to buy drugs and alcohol.

WHO:

1. Since some relationships must be put-off permanently while other relationships may only require a temporary put-off, you must put-on relationships that are more healthy and drug free. Be sure to replace a relationship with a new one with the intent for it to be permanent; however, it may only be temporary as time will tell.

2. Get an accountability partner who can speak the truth in love to you.

3. Get a pastor, elder, or deacon who can be your Bible-teaching "dealer" rather than visiting a drug dealer!

4. Meet new people when you have a friend or relative with you.

5. Call relatives that you may have alienated or avoided in the past because they were "goody two shoes" or "holier than thou" types who did not approve of your partying. These very relatives may become your best relationships.

6. Ask relatives who are Christians to help you by praying for you and to call you to encourage you to stay sober. Humble yourself and confide in them, but use good judgment because not everyone can keep from gossiping.

7. If single, cultivate relationships with the same sex rather than seeking the approval of the opposite sex.

8. Co-workers who encourage Christian living and morals. Associate with them while at work and after work hours in a social setting, but only if allowed by your job's rules.

WHEN:

1. Put-on being alone with God for periods of time of prayer and Bible reading.

2. Put-on spending time with other Christian believers for time of fellowship and encouragement.

3. Put-on feelings of love and acceptance by going to someone when he hurts you directly in order to reconcile the relationship. Be meek, humble, and loving.

4. Fill your most tempting time of the day with a special plan to focus upon helping others and studying/worshiping God (e.g. time of day, seasons, holidays, etc.).

WHY:

1. Joyful mentality must be put-on regardless of your circumstances, trials, problems, and adverse situations. Count it all joy (James 1:2). Also, read Romans 8:28-29.

2. Become balanced in your pessimism (or realism as you probably call it) and be an optimist, too! Again, Romans 8:28-29 comes to mind!

3. Develop a gratitude list or a think list based upon Philippians 4:8-9.[7]

---

[7] Adams, Jay, The Christian Counselor's New Testament, Hackettstown, NJ: Timeless Texts, p. 613.

Divine Intervention

APPENDIX G
RESOURCE LIST AND
RECOMMENDED AUTHORS

While not an exhaustive list, the following authors have materials that can be helpful to you personally and in your efforts to disciple your addicted loved one. Rather than endorse a program of "ten steps" or "eight principles" or the like, I would encourage you to not make it so formal and to view it as a life-long, discipleship process of growing in the Christ-likeness.

Like any good diet plan for eating, the effective plan for overcoming addiction is to change the entire thinking process and lifestyle of the addict rather than to implement a "crash course diet plan" to lose weight but then to gain it all back once the diet is abandoned. Many of those diets are unhealthy anyway and often they are only temporary solutions to a problem of the heart [motives, desires of the inner being].

For this reason, keep the addict reading, writing, and sharing his/her faith with others. Require Bible study, corporate worship, prayer, and fellowship along with books from the following persons:

Jay Adams	Martha Peace
John Piper	Nancy Leigh DeMoss
Wayne Mack	Elyse Fitzpatrick
John MacArthur	Jerry Bridges
Howard A. Eyrich	Stuart Scott
Kent Hughes	Richard Ganz
Don Bowen	Ted Tripp
David Powlison	Larry Burkett
A.W. Tozer	James MacDonald
Mike Cleveland	

For more recommended resources, go to www.nanc.org and click on "resources."

Divine Intervention